THE LORD OF
CONFUSION

THE LORD OF CONFUSION

Ladislas M. Orsy, S.J.

DIMENSION BOOKS
Denville, New Jersey

Published by Dimension Books, Inc.

Denville, New Jersey

Grateful acknowledgement is hereby made to *Sisters Today* and *America* for permission to reprint in revised form in this book articles which they published. Excerpts from *The Jerusalem Bible*, copyright 1966 by Darton, Longman & Todd Ltd. and Doubleday & Company, Inc. Used by permission of the publishers.

Library of Congress Catalog Card Number 74-139814

ISBN: 0-87193

THE LORD OF
CONFUSION

CONTENTS

THE
LORD OF CONFUSION

A lament travels through the Church and fills the four corners of the earth: *There is so much confusion!* It is true. Order is disintegrating; there is much confusion. We are as bewildered as someone who is used to the neat pattern of highways and suddenly finds himself in the jungle. We do not know in what direction to turn; the stars are of little help when the undergrowth blocks our way. We sigh and pray that the road should be clear and that the people of God could march again, singing happy amens and alleluias to the rhythm of one drum.

Yet in God's Kingdom there is time for order and there is time for confusion. Of course order is good. But we were so captivated by its goodness that we excluded all happy confusion as unbefitting the divinity. Thus God became the Lord of order, pure and simple.

From order in nature we concluded that God must exist, and we explained away all disorder that would soil the perfect plan of the Creator. Through the centuries we created a uniform liturgy and we

11

were convinced that God enjoyed our well-ordered services. We built up a great body of canon law that provided an answer to most of our questions and smoothed our insecurities with the clarity and certainty of a great system. Popes, bishops, pastors and layfolk dedicated themselves to this pursuit of order. There was a clear answer to every obscure question; someone only had to find it. Christians could sail towards heaven in a channel clearly marked with colored buoys and flashing lights.

Now all that is over. There is no order; confusion reigns supreme. There may be colored buoys on the sea but no one knows how to interpret them. There may be flashing lights but no one can read them. We are lost on the sea, tossed about by the waves. When will it all end?

Let us say first and comfortingly that the confusion is not absolute. Great it is, no doubt, but parallel with it our fundamental certainties remain. The main signals are there. The Church has not lost its faith; the Creed is sung all over the earth. The faith of the Christians in their Lord is manifest in quiet assumptions, in forceful prayer, in loving deeds that no one can question.

Then let us admit that there is plenty of disorder and uncertainty. Consequently, many good Christians wish and work for a return to quieter times.

And it is true that in many things we need a better balance than we have. Yet I trust God will not listen to their prayers fully. If we need some order, so we need some confusion. To be a Christian is to build *some* order and to live with confusion. We must seek our security elsewhere and in other ways than we did in the past. Our God may be the God of order; he is also and by equal right the God of confusion.

Did not our God create the jungle? The small mind of man would have planted all the trees in geometric patterns, the tall ones on the north, the small on the south. Do the stars in the sky follow any pattern? Had they been planted by man, the crooked line of the Big Bear would not be there; it would be straight.

The jungle and the stars speak of an artist who shaped the universe with sovereign liberty and delighted himself in millions of shapes, sizes and colors. Above all, God left his creature man, created to be free and intelligent, to struggle painfully toward consciousness and the discovery of fire. Creation was marked by purpose and confusion. Yet, if there was chaos there was also the Spirit of God who imprinted beauty and movement into all things.

Neither did Christ leave a theological handbook to his disciples. How much struggle he would have spared his Church if he, from the beginning, had only made the doctrine of the Trinity clearer. He did not. He left his Church for some seven centuries the prey of confusion and misunderstanding, due partly to the lack of precise concepts in the

Gospel. But the Spirit of Christ was with the Church all through those centuries. And eventually a reasonable clarity about the existence of the great mystery was achieved.

Nor did Christ hand over a book of laws to his disciples, with all the precepts for virtuous living and with a classified list of mortal and venial sins. He was too much poet and artist to do any such thing.

But he was also a man with a heart full of compassion. He knew our anxieties and our need for security. He provided for his confused people. He gave them his Spirit to be with them, to help them and to guide them. He did not give them ultimate clarity in theology, nor did he give them a book of laws. He left the disciples with the goodness of his simple words and with much potential confusion. But he sent a loving person to take care of them.

Insecurity and obscurity are part of our human and Christian condition. We have to live with them. Let us pray the Lord, therefore, that he should not take them away. Let us pray rather for the grace of confidence when we walk in the jungle or when we sail on the high seas.

We must understand that God is not just pure intellect or sovereignly strong will; he is also a poet who likes the dancing rhythm of words even when the meaning gets somewhat confused. He is a musician, too, who loves the play of sounds even when to interpret them rationally is baffling or impossible. And he is a painter who likes to throw strong colors on a canvas and enjoy the effects, although those who look at it may think the painting is upside down.

If our God is the Lord of confusion, as much or more than the Lord of order, we simply cannot have a neatly ordered and predictable liturgy all the time. God would not enjoy it. We cannot have a Church with prompt theological answers for all situations. Nor can we have a book of laws that would remain in an unchangeable order. The Pilgrim Church should not be marching to the rhythm of one drum; it should make its way in many groups of pilgrims each singing its own melody, all of them going in the same direction with the somewhat dissonant harmony of one song: *Give Praise to the Lord, Amen, Alleluia.*

We do not trust in order but in the Spirit who leads God's pilgrims through all confusion.

WHO IS A TRUE
PROPHET?

The voice of the prophet is as good for our society as the fresh wind of spring for pollution-filled Manhattan. People on the streets are chilled by it, but once the smoke and the fog are blown away and the salty scent of the ocean is felt there is a quiet exhilaration in the crowds. Everybody breathes deeper and walks more vigorously. When the prophet speaks, his word grips our innermost being and cleanses it. After the first shock we begin to live with a new zeal. Without fresh wind Manhattan would be suffocating; without prophets our society would decay.

But how to know a true prophet from a false one? How to know who is sent by God and who is merely a self-appointed town crier?

The ancient Israelites already had that problem. They asked for proofs when someone claimed that he was a prophet. Without fail, those who were sent by Yahweh had the capacity to produce signs: their credentials were in order. The prayer of Elias brought down fire on the sacrificial offerings, while the priests of Baal had no answer from heaven through their shouting. Israel learned who the true prophet was.

The signs of today may not be so dramatic. But we still need signs. How can we open ourselves to God's disturbing message through a prophet unless we know he is really sent to us? How can we reject the half-truth or the misleading words of those who have no business to prophesy unless we can check their credentials? Right discernment is capital for the health of our society. Salty air should not be confused with carbon monoxide. The one heals, the other kills.

Discernment is a complex art. There is no single test to identify God's man, but there can be a convergence of unobtrusive signs that give enough certainty to discern the message. Ultimately, the Holy Spirit in the heart of every Christian will give final witness to the truth of the prophet's message. We do something less: we are concerned with the signs that are identifiable by thoughtful observation and reflection.

A true prophet is marked more by the capacity to listen than by the ability to speak. Nothing surprising in this, although it sounds unusual. Ordinarily we associate prophets with speaking. But we should recall that before he can speak the message he must hear it. Those who cannot listen cannot carry a message. A fundamental quality in a true prophet, therefore, is the capacity to give himself to another through generous, unprejudiced listening. He must be an intellectually open person, eager to hear unexpected and surprising news — to be transmitted to others.

A prophet is internally strong. He can hear any opinion. He can even cheerfully debate it because he has a certainty about his own message. He knows whom he believes in. This quality of openness must be manifest in daily life. One who cuts off his fellow man cannot listen to God either. Nor is God likely to choose him. He would rush away with half the message and bring havoc on the community.

The true prophet is a man whose heart is full of love. He wants to build a new society. He knows that nothing will hold it together except love. He is not a man of hate. He loves everyone and hates no one. When hate appears in the speech of a crier, let us be wary of following him. That hate certainly does not come from God. A neatly disinguishable false element is there, and it makes the whole message suspicious. The universal commandment of love promulgated by Christ applies to all prophets.

The true prophet is burdened by a mystery. He carries a message that is beyond his own vision and performs a task that is above his own strength. In spite of his certainty he knows his inadequacy.

Therefore, there is a certain air of humility around him. This sense of inadequacy can lead to fear; even to desperate evasions.

Many of the great prophets of Israel at one time or another tried to run away from Yahweh. He caught up with them, of course. He found the fleeing Elias under the juniper tree in the desert and brought him back. He visited Jeremiah in his despair and lifted his heart up. Perhaps it would be too much to say that all true prophets try to run away, or try to flee their task at one time or another, or that they go through periods of depression. Yet, if there is a prophet who never experiences any of this we have to watch out. If he does not feel the burden of mystery he is not likely to have it. The message, therefore, may not be the Word of Yahweh, but a flight of fancy.

Prophets can have different styles. Some of them are called to shout, some to whisper. One can be like the roaring wind, the other like the gentle breeze. There are messages that must be shouted on the streets whether the passers-by listen or not. Jeremiah was unfortunate enough to be chosen for such a task. Israel needed strong medicine in those days. There are messages, too, that must be conveyed with tenderness and sensitivity, without hurting or shocking. Such messages are strengthening like good food. They come through gentle persons. The book of Isaiah records many comforting and delicately beautiful speeches.

It follows, then, that when we are looking for signs of prophetic speech the roaring wind should not have the monopoly. Certainly there can be prophetic speech shouted on the streets, but there can also be prophetic whispers uttered in the kitchen by a Christian mother to the benefit of her children. Since Jesus' style was a subdued one in comparison with some of the Old Testament prophets, one is led to suspect that in this Christian age there is more prophecy by whisper than by declamation.

The age of prophets is certainly not gone. It is with us perhaps more than ever before. After all, Christ brought us a new abundance and his message has spread all over the earth. We should be good enough to listen to the voice of men sent by God and shrewd enough to close our ears to deceptive tales. None of the signs described above is infallible. But all signs put together can give a good indication where the voice comes from. The ultimate discernment will be given by the Holy Spirit in a way that no author is competent to describe.

MOON JOURNEY AND
THEOLOGICAL METHOD

Precision is the key to success in applied sciences and the precision that scientists have achieved is astonishing. We have seen it at work when we watched the marvelous feat of the re-entry of the astronauts into the atmosphere of the earth. The space capsule, so we were informed, had to aim home at a well-determined angle with little margin left for error. A re-entry one degree lower would have caused the capsule to bounce back into space on a senseless journey without destination. A re-entry one degree higher would have generated such heat by friction that the capsule would have burned up and fallen apart like a shooting star.

Since so much is at stake in space navigation no wonder that it takes long to train a pilot or a navigator for a space ship. No well meaning amateurs or daring adventurers are allowed anywhere near the complex machine. The screening process of the candidates makes it sure that a superficially inclined person does not make the grade. For the time being space travel is for professionals only.

In fact, there is a built-in penalty in applied sciences against ignorance or incompetence. A small error in mathematical calculations may endanger the safety of many persons. A slight carelessness in the structure of some component material may lead to a disastrous explosion.

Nature does not readily tolerate stupidity. If someone tampers with its laws it reacts violently. Such a reaction is usually enough to keep off incompetence.

It may sound surprising, but theologizing is hardly less delicate an art than to work in the field of science. Facts have to be ascertained with care and exactitude. After all, a theologian is expected to reflect on God's saving deeds in history. So he must know what happened and know it with as much precision as the human mind allows. He must begin with ascertaining facts as a scientist does. Then the theologian has to articulate his perception through human concepts, an impossible task since the deeds of God do not fit well into the categories of man. Yet a task to be attempted. The results are our clumsy terms, such as trinity, grace, sacraments, for overwhelming mysteries. The balancing of these little words against the great mysteries is a feat that even St. Paul felt to be too much for him. In a way a scientist is in a better position than a theologian. He knows what he is talking about.

Once the concepts are formed judgments have to be made: judgments approximating truth and tentatively or definitely excluding falsity, also exploring relations among mysteries. A mental process not quite dissimilar to the working hypotheses of the scientist. Finally, the results have to be communicated to others who have their own categories, philosophies and general world views. Unless the theological statements are adapted to this audience they will be lost in the process of communication. The scientists have a comparable problem. They do not find it easy to talk to laymen.

No wonder it takes a lot of training to be a good theologian. Facts have to be studied, a capacity to articulate the right questions and to find answers has to be developed. The art of good communication has to be learned.

It would follow that the number of good theologians is as restricted as the number of good scientists. Yet is this true? Scientists seem to be rare and few, but legion is the name of theologians. Few are those who discuss atomic theories but many are those who argue theological hypotheses. Only the brave write scientific articles, but to publish in theology becomes an ordinary enterprise. Do we really have so many competent persons? Perhaps we do, perhaps we do not.

There are some differences between science and theology that make it easier to venture into the field of theology. There is no built-in immediate penalty in theological endeavor. If someone makes a colossal mistake nothing explodes. In fact, he might be catapulted into fame since his theory is new, different and daring. Eventually the professionals will catch up with the amateur and the bright star may disintegrate into lifeless pieces. But it all takes time, sometimes decades, even centuries. Hence amateurs can keep on working for quite a while.

Moreover, to speak in a sensible way about science some basic knowledge of it is necessary, a knowledge not easy to acquire. That is the reason why a layman is reduced to silence at a gathering of scientists. It is not just a question of jargon, it is a question of erudition and training. But, let us admit, many persons have a basic knowledge of theology. It is not sufficient to start them on the path of critical reflection as we described it, but just enough to inspire them with interesting hypotheses, rooted not so much in reality as in a blessedly fertile imagination. Such a gift may lead to interesting articles and apparently epoch-making books — within the field of theology fiction. Because it is difficult to come to grips with the fundamental laws of science there are no instant scientists. But because the facts about God's revelation are communicated to many, the danger of instant theology exists; more plainly, instant theologians are speaking and writing.

In fact, we have an over-abundance in theological literature today; yet learning and wisdom, side by side with depth, are as rare as ever. There is a cult of superficial questions and easy solutions, perhaps more than ever in our history.

A secure touchstone of a good theologian is that he is eager to learn God's ways among men but slow to impose his opinions about transcendent mysteries. A good theologian spends much time in reflection; even when he speaks after a long silence, you feel that he would prefer to listen. There is no substitute for the long and arduous process of learning, be it in science, be it in theology. For the right answer the question must hit the topic at the right angle.

STRUCTURES, AUTHORITY

AND ALL THAT

The human spirit should soar free; there should be no law for art, for poetry or for those supreme manifestations of human genius that create new things from old. The spring of life is inside men's minds and hearts; no external barrier should crush it or limit it. Moreover, when the Spirit of God chooses to be with man's own spirit, man's freedom becomes imperative to such a degree that no human law can hamper it or even regulate it. Who can set norms for the Spirit of God or for his prophets?

Yet in the Church we are beset with institutions and structures. Wherever we look they are there. Near at home there is the parish and the ubiquitous convent. Not so far there is a monastery and, for good measure, a Jesuit college. Over all of them presides the diocesan chancery and the bishop;

they are forcefully evident. The bishops' confer-
ence may look remote and the papacy distant until
their statements and rules touch our life. Admittedly, the institutional structures in the Church can
be overwhelming, not to say suffocating.

At times it seems that we are betraying the Spirit
for the sake of a perfectly organized society. We
make our spirit and God's prisoners in the cage of
our norms and laws.

Agreed, the balance between spirit and structures in the Church is disturbed, and what we have
at present does not suit our age. It follows that we
should aim at and work for a better harmony between the two. It does not follow that we have to
drop all external structures. To abandon them
would mean to relinquish our humanity. We need
institutions as much as our body needs a bone
structure. It is a human need. Even the ineffable
inspiration of God needs the human words of the
prophet to communicate it. The music born in the
mind of a composer needs an instrument to delight
us with a symphony.

We need structures because we need community. Mankind's most desperate need today is to heal
its divisions and to form one community. With our
expeditions to the moon, the earth has become too
small for murderous rivals, for nations antagonized
by hate. The Church, too, if it wants to be a sign
to all nations, has to be the people to whom one
can point saying: "Look how much they love each
other."

Now community means unity, unity of minds and hearts, one vision in many minds, one purpose in many hearts. This cannot be achieved unless there is a center of unity in the group where all the ideas and aspirations converge and are woven into one, and then are proposed in the name of the whole community. This center of unity that makes possible for many to be one in mind and heart is what we call authority. Authority is the living center of unity. The greatest authority is Christ; is he not the center of our unity for all our history? In a community we need authority because without it there is no center and source of unity. If there is no source of unity, there is no movement either. Where there is no movement there is no life. Authority, therefore, is the condition, source and creator of unity that is essential for a community.

We are just explaining the laws of human communities; there is nothing particularly Christian in our reasoning. Yet our reasoning applies to the Christian Church as well. God accepted our human condition and made it part of his own plans. He wanted a group of people that was more than a loose group of believers; he wanted a community. Hence there had to be centers of unity in the Church. And there are. In the diocese it is the bishop; in the universal Church it is the pope. To be a center of unity is really a humble condition; one has to listen to everybody and to speak to the whole community. And to make sure about this lowliness, God leaves them all, pope and bishops, in their human condition. While they serve the unity of the Church, they do not necessarily have the deepest insights into the Gospel nor do they always act in the best possible way. The graces of the deepest wisdom and the highest prudence may be given to any of the members.

The charism of the episcopate is to bring together the aspirations and actions of many and keep them all faithful to Christ and his teaching. They can never function well unless the members of the Church take on the responsibility to inspire them and to help them in their task.

Structures belong to our humanity, like the bones to our body. And Christ wanted structures and institutions. The Spirit soars best when we have all the structures we need, and no more. The more human we are, with the necessary structures, authority and all that, the freer we become and our spirit can soar to the sky.

ON HOPE

For some years we have lived under the shadow of the death-of-God theology. In its extreme form it was something else than *theologizing* since it did not seek an understanding of God's mysteries; rather it called into question God's mighty deeds in our history. To listen to it all was a painful experience for us, the Christian community. No doubt we learned a lot from those authors about our shortcomings in language, in critical research, in naive beliefs; yet, when they reached their radical conclusions the believer's heart froze.

Now the theology of hope is taking over the scene; it is truly the beginning of a new season. It has the warmth and the promise of the spring. In its wake comes a call for celebrating the Lord of life with joyful and playful abandonment.

Hope warms the heart. Man cannot exist without a future. To concentrate on the present only is inhuman. Man needs to dream. The tension between his dream and his present becomes a life-giving force; from such a force new worlds are born.

Christians certainly have a dream, an unreachable and impossible dream: to celebrate life unceasingly for an eternity in the company of the One who gives life.

The dream rests quietly on the fidelity of God who promised us his Kingdom. The dream is more his than ours: he wants us to celebrate life with him. Trust in his fidelity lifts us out of the sorrows and despair of the present world. We have a future; we can hope. And to hope is to live.

The new theology of hope as it unfolds says all this and much more. It struggles a great deal with philosophical foundations. But it focuses on the expectation of the coming of the Lord and the advent of his Kingdom, and on our duty to prepare the earth for it by taking part in all good efforts that build and shape the future. Hope is definitely associated with the future.

Yet Christian hope has another aspect that the new theology of hope does not point out forcefully. Hope springs not only from the expectation of a future gift but from the certainty of a present possession. Christians hope in the coming of the Lord; yet the Lord is already with them. Christians are awaiting the Kingdom; yet the Kingdom is already present to them. A paradox, no doubt. But the second aspect of grounding hope on present possession is just as important as basing it on future expectation.

The victory of Christ over death was also a victory over time. His resurrection is the beginning of a new age where future and present meet, overlap, and co-exist. A situation no man can adequately describe. Only a poet who uses symbolic language or a fool who does not worry about contradictions can convey something of it. The Kingdom is not a future gift really: it is given to us now. We belong to the Risen Christ, we are members of his family. He sends his Spirit and through him the world is re-created. We live in a new creation, we are part of it. So much so that St. Paul was led to exclaim that we already share the glory of the Risen Christ. We are the people in possession. This is what the new theology of hope has not stressed enough as yet.

It follows that there is no point in postponing the celebration of life until Christ comes again. Our hope is a living paradox. It is the expectation of a future gift; yet even more, it is the celebration of a gift already granted. The Kingdom is with us, although not manifest. To hope is to celebrate a present possession rather than to expect a new revelation. Let us, then, happily live hopefully.

THEOLOGY OF BREAD

To enjoy the taste of bread is one of the best gifts man can have. Of course, I am speaking of a rare kind of bread, difficult to find today. You have to search for it. I know it is sold in the Bronx, in a small Italian bakery. The master-baker there has not lost anything of the skill that he inherited from his father who learned it in the old country. Or you may find it in a monastery where goodness has a rich meaning applied even to bread-making. Or you may come across it in a Midwestern farm where the high ideals of the grandmother about how to feed her family have not been eroded by the generation gap. You may find this bread in health shops, too, sitting somewhat uneasily between carrots and Moroccan spices. This is the sort of bread I am speaking about, untouched by automation.

There is something wondrous in the taste of bread. It is so ordinary yet it is so good. It is very democratic. It nourishes the poor and the rich. It goes well with meat or fish, with fruit or cheese. It may return three times a day to the table; it may even stay there all day long. Yet it never outstays its welcome.

True, we would not want to live merely on bread all the time. We put butter on it; a great improvement. If you top the butter with honey, you have a dessert worthy of the table of a medieval king. In other terms, the ordinary taste of bread has to be refreshed with extraordinary additions. From time to time we need celebrations. On rare occasions we have an elaborate banquet. But after one or two rich meals we are saturated and we long for the simple taste of bread again. Granted we need festivities; but if there is a feast every single day there is no celebration ever.

The philosophical conclusion is that we need ordinary things, such as bread, to sustain life in us through a quiet and peaceful taste that can be relished over and over again. If the ordinary is there, there is a good foundation for feasts and celebrations.

To destroy our taste of the ordinary is to interfere with the foundations of our life. We need much peaceful monotony to enjoy surprising happenings. At the time of monotony the spirit of the inner man awakes. Not distracted, he can reflect on himself and on the outside world. The quiet rhythm of the ordinary is the best framework for thinking in depth. Great deeds and movements never originated in shallow thoughts; all giant trees have deep roots. If they do not, the first wind blows them over. Someone who wants to celebrate all the time will keep his spirit captive.

Time has come to write the theology of the ordinary. It should be the theology of simple meals, steady work, peaceful walks, and relaxing conversations. Then it should move to reflect on ordinary worship, simple liturgies that should surround the bread and wine that is offered on our altars. Even in worshiping God we cannot live on an exciting and a newly created celebration every day for the same reason that we cannot have an elaborate banquet every day. If we did we would destroy the feasts altogether.

There should be no misunderstanding. We certainly want creativity. But periods of calm and reflection and the ordinary rhythm of everyday life are needed for creativity that springs from genuine depth. From time to time we need new prayers in unexpected and surprising forms; much of the time we need the repetition of familiar words so that our minds and hearts could be freed from concentrating on words and forms and could surrender to a movement of faith and love that is beyond any human expression.

To enjoy the unusual we must have a steady taste for the usual. To enjoy a great banquet we must appreciate the daily bread. This paradox is found in the Gospels too. Jesus promises to his faithful disciples a heavenly banquet. Yet while they are waiting for it he taught them to pray for their daily bread.

TO DISCOVER THE
PRESENCE PLEASE
WATCH THE PROCESS

The bishops assembled at council declared solemnly and we all believe that the Church is a sign of God's saving presence among men. The declaration caused as much joy as pain. The joy was immediate; it came from the fulfillment of an expectation. The council clearly recalled the old truth: the Church does not exist for itself but for all men. The phrase about *sign* was effective; it knocked down many walls fast and put an end to centuries' long isolation. Rightly so. Sign means communication.

The pain was slower to be felt, but it is increasingly there. It is growing sharper to the point of agony. The sign does not stand up to examination. If the Church is a sign of God's presence, it must be filled with peace, beauty and holiness. In fact, we are divided. We carry on our ugly arguments about small domestic problems. Sins abound in the midst of the chosen people. These would be forgivable if the hierarchy at least were consistently wise, farsighted and charismatic. But our bishops, too, seem to have their fair share of human limitations. Then there are impersonal structures and proceedings; they turn Christ's warm love into cold justice — after years of delay.

The great vision of the council was a collective dream in which the bishops indulged within the splendor of St. Peter's Basilica. It is contradicted by hard facts.

The contrast between the ideal and the real creates tensions and crises in the community. The reactions and responses vary. There is the preacher who shuts his eyes to the real situation and harangues his congregation about the Church that is the spotless bride of Christ and the perfect community. All wrongs are attributed to the ubiquitous presence of the devil who appears to be more active today than ever before. Then there is the radical reformer who flatly declares that the Church is corrupt to the point of being a counter-sign: a sign that says the Kingdom is elsewhere. All good things really happen outside the Christian community. Between the pious preacher and the radical reformer there is the multitude of believers.

Many of them are bewildered, lost and hungry. They cannot follow either of the two extremes. They know the Church cannot be all holiness; facts and common sense are against such a position. They cannot accept either that there is no holiness in the Church; they experience it publicly and secretly more than once. Between frequent barrages of words from both sides, they long for light that brings a better vision. After all, if the Holy Spirit was poured out on the Christian community and remains with it, the same community must be a sign of the presence of the Spirit. If not, what is the Spirit of God doing among us? Has he lost his power to transform the heart of man?

The Spirit is there and the Church is a sign of his presence. It is a sign of unique character.

To understand the sign let us speak about the presence that it signifies. It is the dynamic presence of a person who heals, redeems and sanctifies the community. In the midst of Christian people a tremendous drama is enacted. Light comes into the darkness and there is a clash between the two. Good seed is sown and then struggles to take root on the rocks, among weeds, and in good soil, too. Leaven is injected into the mass and the forces of fermentation take over.

The presence is an active one that transforms the community. There is a process with a contrasting beginning and end. The sign of such activity cannot be a clear-cut picture of holiness dropped from heaven, untouched by human hands. The only adequate sign can be the full enactment of a drama, with many personages representing every step in the transformation. The Church is a sign composed of turmoil, struggle, fermentation, brought into this world by the grace of God that through all ages heals, redeems and sanctifies. Unless all those aspects are there the sign would be misleading.

The more we meditate on the Gospel the more it supports us in this interpretation of the sign of God's presence. When John the Baptist in prison sent messengers to Jesus asking if he was the Messiah, Jesus answered: "Go back and tell John what you have seen and heard: the blind see again, the lame walk, lepers are cleansed, and the deaf hear, the dead are raised to life, the Good News is proclaimed to the poor and happy is the man who does not lose faith in me" (Lk. 7:22-23). Jesus refers to a process of transformation: that is, to the sign of a new presence. No wonder that you can expect in the company of Jesus the lame, the blind, and even the dead. Without them we could not see what God's mighty power can actually do. The same pattern repeats itself in the group of the Twelve. First called, they had a long way to go to understand the spiritual nature of the Kingdom. They demonstrated abundantly their lack of understanding. Is there not a transformation of the sons of Zebedee and above all of Peter? This process *is* the sign of a powerful presence.

The pious preacher, of course, does not perceive the sign. He sees only Jesus' gentle goodness and strength. He pretends that all about him were like him. The radical reformer has his eyes locked in on the Twelve who are running for security on the eve of the passion; and he claims this is all that can be seen. Neither of the two knows what makes up the sign. Both are wrong.

The saving deeds of Christ continue in the Church and through the Church. The presence of Jesus' Spirit becomes manifest when men and women are reborn, when they repent of their sins, when they are healed again and again. So many failures, but from death they come to life again to show the power of grace. Sinners, then, are indispensable.

The Church is a sign because light overcomes darkness and because the good seed takes root and the mass is fermented. To discover the presence please watch the process. Do not hold against the community that there are so many blights, frail reeds and fruitless trees among it. But for them the power of God's grace would never be known.

IN PRAISE OF FOOLS

The institution of fools was of capital importance in the courts of kings, princes and even bishops in the Middle Ages and later. The ostensible role of the fool was to entertain all and sundry. But beyond that he had another part to play: to tell the truth in a cheerful way. He could roam around free; he had access to the king and to the kitchen. He was distinguished by the dress of the clown. Under such disguise he could dispense truth and foolishness. He could tell the king what he thought of his government, and no offense was taken since it came from the fool. The head of an ordinary gentleman would have rolled long before had he said the same things.

The world is all the poorer for the lack of fools. On the political scene we have no one to stand in fancy dress before kings and princes, presidents and cabinets ministers, and dispense truth to them in the midst of laughter. Truth can be cruel, but not when it comes from the fool. Yet it can still penetrate deep — because it is the truth.

For this lack of fools our debates take a serious turn and our politicians make solemn statements and scathing speeches. Editorials are written with pomp and acidity. And since there is no good humor around to usher in wisdom, even when wisdom comes it is easily rejected.

Among Christians the situation is not much better. They seem to suffer from a chronic lack of a sense of humor. Perhaps it all originates in the fact that there is among them a chronic lack of peaceful contemplation. Only a contemplative person has the leisure to measure things as they are. He has time to marvel at the immensity of the ocean and admire the clumsy grace of the lobster. He knows the true measure of things; hence he can indulge in laughter when things get out of proportion. He feels the length of time that stretches from our cloudy beginnings to the haze of eternity. He laughs when someone exalts the present moment beyond measure, disclaiming the past and uttering the last word in progress. Much progress is to come. He laughs when in unending space someone claims to be the center of the universe.

If our liturgy is revised and we are going to have new prayers for the Church, perhaps a petition could be inserted: "From those who take themselves too seriously: deliver us, O Lord." And then another: "The grace of good cheer: grant your people, O Lord." How many problems would be resolved if those who are facing each other could see their own limitations in time and space. If they could open their hearts to the immensity of God and the greatness of the Christian people and to all the riches that the future brings, they would laugh good-humoredly at themselves and many of their problems.

I do not suggest that popes and bishops should revive the institution of domestic fools: they might be misunderstood if they did. Our atomic age has little patience for the graceful poetry of the wise fool.

Yet there are many religious communities looking for new ways to serve God and man. Could they make a breakthrough and serve us all as wise fools? They have the wit and wisdom and, God knows, there is need for such new apostolates.

PHILOSOPHY OF WINE

You have to be a recent immigrant to the USA to appreciate the rich potentialities of the land and the fundamental goodness of the people who settled on it. Admittedly, there are violent demonstrations; but progress to maturity was never without turbulence. Europe has known much more of it in the course of its history.

Above all there is a dynamism here that is a sign of life. There is also an eagerness to study and to learn new things: a sign of humility. In fact, the positive values far outweigh the negative ones. Hope is stronger in this land than despair. The people who built a continent out of the wilderness in so little time, and the nation that recovered from the emotional and physical ravages of the Civil War has still much to give to the world.

Yet there is trouble. And, of course, the causes are manifold. Some of them will require radical remedies: experts will have to work on them and students will have to push for them. I have no intention to pinpoint them all or to note priorities. How could anybody do that? But I can single out one source of evil to which a remedy could be applied to the profit of the nation.

One root of our trouble is that Americans do not drink wine; and when they do they do not take wine-drinking seriously enough.

Wine had a place of pride in the Bible. You remember the dramatic story of Noe; how he apparently discovered it and paid some price for enjoying it. The Book of Books abounds in describing friendly vineyards full of peace, song and love to the point that the sign of the destruction of the nation is when those vineyards are destroyed. Praise is given to the wine, a kind and gentle drink making the heart happy. In the New Testament wine is associated with bread and they together make the food that sustains us. The daily bread and the daily wine to lift up our hearts become signs of God's presence among us.

Now wine is a gentle drink indeed. You cannot just gulp it down; you have to savor it, enjoying both its scent and its taste. Wine does not give you a kick (whose spirit was ever lifted up by a kick?) but its effect grows on you until the heart is warmed and the speech becomes spiced with cheer and truth. There is an infinite variety of taste in it. You can and you should have different types of wine from day to day. Every vintage has its own personality: one sweet, the other dry, one heavy, the other light. One for fish, the other for meat, one to be served chilled, the other tasting the best when it has the temperature of your room.

You see how much quiet taste and art goes into wine-drinking. It is, in fact, such a subtle art that you cannot enjoy it without friends. Wine is a democratic drink; it brings people together in quiet conversation. Put on the table a good strong bottle of red wine with some mature cheese and you will have a kingly lunch for rich and poor together.

Good wine-drinking habits are, of course, the greatest enemy of narrow nationalism. Was there a border that at one time or another was not crossed by barrels or bottles, carrying the precious liquid extracted from grapes?

It takes a thoughtful man to drink wine; and to drink wine is conducive to quiet thoughtfulness. This is precisely one thing America needs to do to strike at a root of its evils: quiet thoughtfulness. We need thoughtfulness about revising the international aims of the country. It becomes increasingly clear that the evils of this globe are not cured by bombs. Bombs leave wounds and sad memories that work later for greater disunity among men. It becomes increasingly clear that hunger and poverty are alleviated but not cured by handing out food and money. The dignity of man has to be built up and this requires a thoughtful approach because man is a more complex creature. The coming years will make it clear too that the more violence occurs at university campuses, the lower the academic standards will be. Intellectuals dedicated to thought (usually non-violent people) will quietly leave the disturbed campuses.

If we got together more over wine and cheese to think about our problems and we honestly searched for the solution instead of reacting violently, one root of evil would be gradually extirpated. America is starving for quiet thought, peaceful conversation, even for quiet contemplation. And there is no solution to the evils until the nation finds its soul in peace, poor and rich, black and white, meeting over a glass of wine.

A QUESTION

OF SURVIVAL

A few years ago when concerned Christians met to discuss the state of their Church an easy certainty prevailed among them. It was the kind of certainty a doctor may have at the bedside of a patient whose disease is no match for modern medicine: he knows the crisis will be weathered. Yet, at times the predictions of physicians are wrong; a new virus appears and the challenge of an ordinary disease becomes a question of survival. Today when concerned Christians meet there is much doubt among them, depressing questions are whispered discreetly, or even asked loudly: Shall the Church survive?

The loose talk in the press about a post-Christian era, or about humanism without Christianity, or about Christianity without religion does not help to improve the general mood. As always at times of gloom, well-meaning preachers appear and harangue their listeners that we have to fight and fight hard for the future of the Church. A few years ago we spoke of an illness that would certainly be weathered; now it is a question of survival.

If the wise rabbi Gamaliel, immortalized in the Acts of the Apostles, lived today, he would be quietly amused by these concerned Christians, who, stone-faced and humorless, are battling for survival. He would shake his head and profer again his simple wisdom: "Don't worry," he would say, "if the Christian community is of human origin it will disintegrate of its own accord, your fight for its survival notwithstanding. If the community is God's own doing, it will survive without your gloomy fight."

It is humiliating to listen to Gamaliel at a distance of more than 1900 years. Yet he should know; he made that prophecy once and it worked. When an institution is as absurd as the Christian Church (built on the greatest paradox man ever heard of, that God was made man), it must either disappear or have some divine help to survive. If it has divine help (the fact of survival is a powerful argument for it) no man can save it or damn it.

Concerned Christians need quiet faith and much humility. The Church they are worried about is not theirs, it is Christ's. They are simply not invited to decide about the survival of the Church. That question has been settled long ago, on the shore of the Lake of Genesareth, and on the day when the Spirit was poured out on the Twelve. God will not abandon his people; and there will always be a people for him. His delight is to be with man. And who can deprive God of his good pleasure?

Does it follow that God does not need our help to build his Church? Not at all. In this order of the world he can hardly do without our work.

It sounds all contradictory, but upon reflection, our God is the Lord of surprises and we can best speak about him in paradoxes and contradictions.

Granted, the survival of the Church depends on the fidelity of God. A covenant assuring us of this fidelity has been concluded in the person of Christ. God has no choice now, he has to carry out his promise.

But he needs our help to fulfill his promise. The Good News cannot be spread without preachers. The sacraments cannot be given without men. Without human words and hands the visible and tangible gestures of Christ cannot be repeated throughout history. This is not Pelagianism; just simple, plain truth. God so ordered the world that without our cooperation his mighty deeds of salvation would be of no visible effect.

In a way it is true that the survival of the Church rests with man. It is true that God begs for our services. Without them he would not have a people who know him, love him, and worship him. He would become an unknown divinity, somewhere out there.

It is also true that he does not need any bitter fighter for his Kingdom. Christ told Peter to put away the sword and not to protect his master in a violent way. The Father had other plans for Jesus than to save him by Peter's efforts.

The survival of the Church is the fruit of grace that works in an unexpected way in many hearts and produces surprising results. This happened so many times in the course of history; when shall we be shrewd enough to learn about God's ways from the past? The survival of the Church through the barbaric ages and the collapse of the Roman Empire and through the turmoil of the great migrations of peoples was due to a large extent to the monks who once created the strong and rustic beauty of Monte Cassino and later carried the Good News all over Europe. The survival of the Church through the late Middle Ages was helped powerfully by the friars of Dominic and Francis. Their prayer and learning was a cohesive force while a new age was dawning. Later in the beginning of the Modern Age the priests who learned from Ignatius of Loyola how to obey the Holy Spirit did much to strengthen the shaky edifice of the Christian community. Not by way of any military campaign (whenever they tried it they never succeeded) but by teaching their fellow man to pray and to be good in deeds.

Parallel with these great movements there was another one, not less important. The Church grew through that quiet faith and love that fills Christian households. Many mothers and fathers, less famous than many great saints, were equally great builders of the Kingdom of God.

God's Church does not survive through human means. Gamaliel knew that the Church survives through God's fidelity. How good it is to look back after 1900 years and to see that God proved himself faithful in history. If the Church had been a human institution it would have come to an end long ago. All the human efforts of Christians in nineteen centuries are not an adequate explanation for the survival of the Church. Even today if an outsider looks at our obvious confusions and inefficiencies he easily concludes that we are on our way out from the scene of history. We would be, of course, were it not for the Holy Spirit who keeps the whole institution, pope, bishops, priests and layfolk, all of them included, going. And in this process, the One who told us to think of ourselves as useless servants begs for our services through the gentle action of the Spirit.

Remember the Apostle Paul about 50 A.D.? He could have spoken about a crisis of survival. He must have felt the crushing weight of the pagan world around him, pressing down on the small, budding communities. Yet he never speaks of survival. His mind was filled with the vision of the Risen Lord and his heart was captivated by the unfolding mystery of God's love in human history.

He experienced a wondrous intoxicating expectation. A typical Christian way of life.

WHO MAKES A
GOOD FOOL?

A community that constitutionally establishes the office of the fool takes a great step forward; nay, a leap into the future. The members commit themselves to listen to someone who in his turn is committed to impartial and objective truth. To follow the truth is to march right into the future, without following any crooked line, since no falsity can stand up for long through the storms of history. Therefore, commitment to progress means to have a good fool around.

Yet precautions are necessary. Dedication to the cause of truth does not make a person infallible. Indeed, there is no more dangerous person than the one who is convinced of both the truth of his opinion and the infallibility of his vision. Once the question of the office of the fool is settled and accepted, therefore, great care should be exercised in choosing the right man. Otherwise, a good beginning may come to a sorry end.

So the question comes up: who makes a good fool? Foolery is an art; it is not for the incompetent. Qualified persons are hard to come by. And even when they take office they must be watched. To make the choice right and to compel the fool to live up to the exacting standards of his job, some of the requirements may usefully be listed.

No man can be a good fool unless he can sail the ocean alone. Now the point is not in saying that sailors only are qualified to be fools. The real meaning of the statement is that no one can commit himself to the truth unless he has the capacity to sail alone. In our society many issues are treated politically. Leaders with persuasive voices form parties and try to entice the citizens to support them. The temptation for politicians to use the fool to their gain will always be great. Some will say: "Our position is so right that even the fool is with us." Or, "Look at the other party; only the fool is with them." Yet in reality the path of the fool must be a lonely one without concession to the right or the left. He should not battle his way; that is definitely not his role. His progress is more like that of a gentle sailboat with funny designs on the canvas. Because he cannot and should not expect support from anyone, his internal strength should be well above the average.

No man can be a good fool unless he has the ca-

pacity to dream beyond his knowledge. A difficult quality to formulate. Let us explain it. The fool should distance himself from his own age. He should know what happened in the past so that he could advise his own contemporaries bent on repeating the mistakes of earlier generations. More important though, he must sense the fleeting value of the present moment. There was no age in the past when men were tempted so much to be drunk with their own achievements as our age. We take a few steps on the moon and in our jubilation we forget that there remains a universe, immense beyond any measure, to be explored. We split and we fuse atomic particles and in the glory of our success, surrounded by a mushroom cloud, we forget that we do not know where the particles come from. A good fool should see beyond the present and have an awareness that it will not take fifty years before we will all be old and out-of-date. He should not flatter his contemporaries. He should make them aware that all they can do is to make a little step in the unending process of universal history.

A good fool should love the bitter-sweet taste of the Chinese kitchen. It is easy to like a plain steak. It is not difficult to relish a sweet dessert. The art is in combining the bitter and the sweet. In particular we Americans are inclined to keep the different tastes apart. Our politics and social movements tend to be blunt and bitter with no sweetness added to them. Then, for relaxation we take refuge in watching movies and shows that describe a dream world all sweet with none of the bitterness of real life in it. The good fool integrates society in his own person. The cruelty of the truth and the beauty of the dream meet in his exacting work. That is why good fools cannot last too long. They are burnt up in their pacifying mission: to tell the truth in the midst of laughter.

The good fool learned to laugh with a broken heart. The fool is a man like anyone else in need of sympathy and understanding. But his office displays a glaring contradiction. His dress claims that he should not be taken seriously; his wisdom demands that he should not be dismissed lightly. Such a paradoxical situation opens the door wide and large to all accusations. Those who do not like his fancy robe will call his wisdom phony or just plain folly. Those who do not like his wisdom will not mix with a man in fancy robe. He has no defense against any of them. His good humor and wise words may not be rewarded. No fool will hear frequently the rewarding sound of "Thank you"— such a human need after an honest effort or a good deed. After all, who would thank a fool. Yet deep down, he is no different from others except by his vocation. At times his heart may be broken.

To be a fool is surely a strange call. It defies all definition. Poetry only can do some justice to it.

Who Makes a Good Fool?

And I recall a verse I read in Italian:
When you have lost everything
and have nothing,
but two pieces of bread
left in your pocket:
sell one piece,
and buy a flower for the price you receive
to have some nourishment for your heart.
. . . Who but a fool would do that? . . .

PLAY OR BATTLE?

Play has always fascinated man and defied all classification by scientists — to such an extent that recently a sociologist, Peter Berger (who is also a theologian), lifted play out of all ordinary categories and put it right on the edge of eternity, claiming that through it the rumor of angels is kept alive among men. Play points to a reality that transcends our visible and tangible universe.

There is a particular excitement when play develops into a game, a friendly fight between two opposing parties, measuring their strength on the edge of eternity. This is so good that when a spectacular game is played, a spectacular crowd gathers, too. And they all enter into the same spirit. When the game is on between the Mets and the Cubs, time stops, worldly problems collapse and the rumor of angels is heard all over the stadium. Mankind finds its spirit.

Good as the game is, we have to watch out that it should not be spoiled. The better a thing is, said the ancient philosophers, the worse it turns out if corruption sets into it. Indeed, there is nothing uglier than when spirited play becomes a senseless fight or when a chivalrous game is transformed into a bitter battle.

In the Church the play and games of the theologians could be the rumor of angels for all of us. They are busy about understanding God's mysteries better; there must be ample room there for play. New aspects discovered by different persons may bring all the excitement of a game. We all would be fascinated by watching their exchanges. Did we not recently witness theologians speaking in the market place, drawing crowds?

Yet here and there a sourness invades the debate, the game turns into war; the cheerful match of spirits is imperceptibly transformed into bitter arguments. Parties are labeled and strictly identified. Today the opponents are classified as conservatives and progressives. The division is spreading so far that when someone admits at a cocktail party that he is a theologian he has to identfy himself further as a conservative or progressive, as once Christians and Turks had to identify themselves with designs on their armor. From then on it is a question of loyalty to the cause and to its presumed prophets, with no personal thinking allowed. A war is spreading that will lead to devastation and famine.

But the real split in the Church is not between conservatives and progressives. It runs between those who have an open mind and a willing heart and those who have a closed mind and a frozen heart. This division goes deep and does untold harm.

A person of open mind is always ready to listen and to receive, because he knows he has not reached his ultimate development. A person of closed mind is ready to talk and to give because he thinks he represents the final stage of evolution. A person of willing heart is always ready to take a guide and move ahead, since he senses that there is more that he does not know than that he does know. A person of frozen heart stays in the same place forever, since he is convinced that everybody has to be his disciple.

Only those of open mind and willing heart can build the Church. Those of closed mind and frozen heart paralyze us all.

But let us not be mistaken; the dividing line is not as clear as all that. There are young and old, men and women, layfolk and clergy on both sides. There are open-minded conservatives and frozen-hearted progressives, and vice versa.

Of course, these are simple categories, and really there is openness and closeness in all of us. We serve God and man if we open our mind to new insights and are willing to take the risk of new explorations. Then it does not matter much if one of us is conservative, another progressive. The different opinions will lead to a refreshing game. A theologian who understands our past and loves it, but knows that the work of the Spirit among men has not yet come to an end, is a blessing for the Christian community. A theologian whose intent is on the future work of the Spirit but who knows that light comes from the past, too, is a pioneer of our progress. The game between the two groups — the conservatives and the progressives who both have an open mind and a willing heart — can become once again the rumor of angels in the Church. The People of God and the angels will surely enjoy it.

POLITICS AND CHURCH

Our age is the age of the builders of the earth and the age of pioneers in search of new frontiers. Who could think of a worse attitude than to stand aloof, cool and uncommitted while builders are raising solid structures and gracious arches for the new cathedrals of new generations, and while explorers are pushing their way into the unknown amid thousands of dangers?

This is true on many levels in our society; it is certainly true on the political level. There, new dimensions for the life of society are conceived and new structures are erected to bring us nearer to the golden age of man. Rightly, it seems, Christians are urging their Church not to stand aloof, cool and uncommitted while the fight is on and a new world is emerging. The Church should be in the thick of things, politically involved and committed.

As with so many simplistic statements, this one, too, is pregnant with truth and may give birth to a healthy offspring — but caution is necessary. If the process of birth is not properly assisted, a monster may see the world — or the world may see a monster.

Every Christian should be committed to this quest of building the earth and exploring new frontiers. His commitment should not be undertaken merely because he happens to be interested in engineering or geography. It should be the fruit of his loyalty to Christ, through whom all things are made. To build the face of the earth or to seek new frontiers is to enter humbly into the work of the Son, of the Word, who is the source of life and movement. Politics should not be an exception; man's life can be bettered very much by good politicians. To stand aloof, cool and indifferent in political matters is wrong for a Christian.

To be active in politics is, then, the duty of every Christian. Members of the clergy or of religious communities are not excepted; after all they are citizens. They live in this world even if much of their work is for a future one. They have therefore to share the burden of their fellow man.

Clearly, if every Christian takes this duty seriously, a great variety of views, attitudes and decisions arise. The official Church as far as it is represented by the hierarchy should respect this variety, rejoice in it and stand behind its members — of all opinions. The Church should affirm and defend their right to choose freely what they think is best and should not impose any opinion on them.

The Church should uphold the person who makes the decision, not the decision itself.

But what about the official Church as it is represented by the hierarchy? Should not the official Church enter into the daily struggle of politics and get involved and committed? Is this not part of its mission — to build a new society and seek new frontiers for the human community?

The Church should go into politics, if it can do it well. But can the Church do it well? There is no evidence that Christ or His Spirit ever has given the Church the charism of making good decisions in matters of temporal political situations. There is plenty of historical evidence that whenever the hierarchy has tried to do it the disadvantages outweighed by far, in space and time, the advantages secured. No wonder. The Church simply does not have a gift of prudence that assures that its decisions in political matters are good. The gift of the bishops is that of fidelity in proclaiming the evangelical message, not that of being good at politics.

Individual Christians have to build their lives on the Gospel; they have to apply it in their daily situations. They should be free from interference in this; they are, after all, grown-up persons. The official Church should not get involved in politics because it has no gift for it and will do badly. If it ever gets involved, its pronouncements do not represent more than the human wisdom of the pope, bishops and clergy concerned. And that may or may not be great. In fact, their inexperience in political matters may be the cause of disaster. We should get used to the fact that when the bishops, priests or religious talk about politics they speak their own mind. We should not see in them representatives of the Church. We should accept them as fellow Christians taking their own personal stand, which they have a right to take.

One qualification is necessary, however. When the message of faith, hope and love is trampled on, when justice and fairness are cynically disregarded by so-called statesmen and politicians, then the official Church or the hierarchy has to speak up loud and clear and do whatever is possible to put an end to injustice.

To sum up: The official Church should not get involved in ordinary politics because it has no charism and little earthly wisdom for it. Individual Christians should build the earth and pioneer toward new frontiers via politics whenever it is necessary. The official Church should uphold their right to choose freely, but it should not give them instructions on what to do. Whenever there is injustice in the community the hierarchical Church should speak up against it.

When the clergy and religious speak on everyday politics, they do not represent the Church. We should relieve them of the inhuman burden of speaking in the name of the Church on all things conceivable, and we should grant them the right to speak for themselves.

Did you notice how much this respects the Chirstian person and how little temporal power it attributes to the institutional Church? This may well be the right balance for the future.

COMMITMENT FOR LIFE

The man of ancient ages was fascinated by the world around him. He liked to watch the sky, the ocean and the mountains. He populated them with various gods who had power to rule his life. He was much less interested in himself. His age was not the time of experimental psychology.

With the coming of our modern days man has become fascinated with himself and has started exploring the secrets and mysteries of his own *psyche* and emotions. Kant in philosophy and Freud in psychology are just two leading names who represented the new trend.

No doubt, psychology has made great progress in exploring the obscure roots of our judgments, desires and decisions. Recently, much research was done on the capacity of man to commit himself. In particular, the question was raised if he is able to make a *permanent* commitment, a commitment that is to last for a lifetime.

The result of this inquiry is strongly negative.

The arguments put forward to buttress the conclusions appear convincing.

Man has, the psychologists say, only a limited capacity to comprehend himself and the world around him. All his decisions are made within a very restricted field. He cannot reach beyond his horizon and commit himself to the unknown; all his commitments operate within the field of his perception. Eventually this field enlarges; a person never stops growing. With new knowledge and inspiration new worlds open up to him. In this continuous process there is a need for the re-evaluation of all previous promises.

Further, this process means increased freedom. A commitment for life at any given stage would be equivalent to imprisoning a man. Chained to his narrow past by a promise, he would not have the freedom to make his contribution to the present and to build the future. He would not grow.

These insights from psychology bring an air of exhilaration all around. Young persons must not take on the inhuman burden of determining the course of their whole life with a promise that is binding forever. They must not walk in their prime into the unknown future with their hands tied. Older persons must not feel embarrassed to break their promise if after long experience they know that it was a mistake.

Thus speak the experts in psychology.

Their conclusions touch deeply some Christian

attitudes. Christians formulated their marriage vows for centuries with the clause that the union was to last until man and wife part at death. Young religious, too, bound themselves with great solemnity and awe-inspiring ceremony to an exclusive service of God forever. Should all this continue? Should we not tell them all honestly that in their enthusiasm they are over-reaching themselves?

In honesty, they should be so told. We should not reject the conclusions of science if they are well-founded — and in the present case the arguments appear conclusive.

Yet there is another aspect to it all.

When someone pronounces the marriage vows before God a third person is involved: God himself. He calls the two who love each other to an adventure beyond human strength. This is precisely the Christian dimension of marriage: Christ is involved in it. When a young person dedicates himself to the exclusive service of God in a religious community God is a partner to the adventure; he calls his creature to a life of specific beauty and depth.

The experts may well be right; no man can commit himself for life. But when it comes to an adventure in which God is the main party, the real question is not what *man* can do but how far the strength of *God* can go. And it can go very far. God can commit himself to the life-span of a fragile man — and much beyond it.

Strangely enough, God loves an adventure with man. He called Abraham: "Leave your country, your family and your father's house, for the land I will show you" (Gen. 12:1). The call was a life-long commitment that embraced eventually not only Abraham but his wife and son and all his posterity. It is the exuberance, the abundance of love that makes God commit himself for life-long adventures with man. And the case of Abraham was not unique: other names can be quoted to the same purpose. Yahweh called all the prophets of the Old Testament and he never abandoned them. Later, Jesus chose the Twelve in an exuberance of love and committed himself to them for life and beyond.

The Christian community through the centuries has been aware of God's promises that last longer than man can calculate. Trust in God's fidelity inspired young men and women to commit themselves to each other for a lifetime. Other young men and women dedicated themselves to an exclusive service of God through their religious vows in perpetuity. They all proclaimed their faith in God's fidelity. They were not wrong. The events of their life proved that their trust had not been misplaced, although we have no writings to document it. Quiet strength communicated day by day in an intangible way is not a matter for historians.

In fact, the conclusions of modern psychology coincide with the articulated conviction of many

Christians in the past: man is not strong enough to commit himself for a lifetime. Yet faith has a dimension beyond the reach of psychology. Faith can give the awareness that God is willing to commit himself to man in a specific vocation, be it marriage or religious life. This vision of faith generates hope in God's fidelity. In this perspective of faith and hope the foolish marriage vows of life can be celebrated with music, song and dance. It all makes sense to the believer. Also, religious consecration forever can be enacted with all the solemnity that the local community and Mother Church can provide. The adventure that brought Abraham out of his country and sent him into a new land starts all over again.

When such festivities occur, be it a wedding or a vow day, *all you people clap your hands* and invite the experts in psychology to the banquet they cannot give.

COMMUNITY, SCRIPTURES
AND STRUCTURES

The relationship between the Christian community and the books of the New Testament is more than an interesting theological puzzle; it is a mystery. Since the beginning the Scriptures nourished the life of the community; yet all through history the community was called on to interpret the Scriptures well beyond the literal meaning of the text. The Church drew life from the Bible; the Bible's message developed through the insights of the Church. There *was* and there *is* an interaction, difficult to follow and even more difficult to put into precise laws.

To throw some light on this mysterious relationship should be the primary concern of all theologians since the two important sources that provide them with facts and data for reflection are the Holy Scriptures and the living faith of the community.

Yet, astonishingly, many theologians rush into particular problems and solutions, without any attempt to clarify this basic issue.

Some assume that once we know the full meaning of the texts all our problems are solved. For them, the text of the early Apostolic writings are not so much the beginning of a development as the final stage of an accomplishment beyond which the community should never go. A fascinatingly simple outlook.

Some other theologians do not give much weight to the Scriptures. Its books, they say, are the projection of the faith of the early Christian communities; their writers made a valiant attempt to describe God's revelation to the world surrounding them. The Scriptures are for us more of a distant model than a proximate norm of faith. If they are irrelevant to our historical circumstances we have to look elsewhere for guidance. Another simplification that appeals mainly to those who do not see how much Christianity is rooted in past history.

Somewhere between these two extremes lies the truth. Where exactly we do not know. The balance between past and present, between inspired books written long ago and a community that lives now is so complex and delicate that its full understanding escapes even the best theologians. But we can make good approximations of it.

From the earliest times we find in the community a two-fold action, first the free creation of the

Scriptures and then the reception of them as inspired by the Spirit and having binding force on the community. A surprising combination of attitudes: the community bound itself by what it created. The explanation is that Christians recognized a transcendent force both in the creation and in the reception of those writings. The community believed that the Spirit was with those who composed the documents, and afterwards the same Spirit gave discernment to the community to receive the written texts as normative. In fact, the Scriptures became an immutable guide and norm which generations of Christians had to follow and never depart from.

Yet fidelity did not mean inflexibility. The community soon achieved new insights and understandings, in particular (and not without a major crisis) about the Father and the Son and the Holy Spirit and their relation to each other, or about the mystery of God who became man. New expressions became commonplace; even the ordinary folk spoke of three persons in one God, or two natures in one Christ; a terminology that was not lifted from the books of the New Testament.

In all this process the Scriptures remained a source of inspiration, or guidance, but they did not become a barrier to development. Understandably, the Sacred Writings were not there to strangle the Spirit but to create a favorable atmosphere for the working of the Spirit. The creative capacity of the community has not been taken away. The text of the Scriptures could not be an end, a *terminus* of the process. Rather, it had to create and foster progress.

It is interesting to speculate how far the original creative capacity remained with the Christian community. After all, the light and the strength of the Spirit *is* with it. Admittedly, one movement in God's revelation terminated with the death of the last Apostle; but another movement is alive since the Spirit is leading us all the time to a better vision of the truth. What could the community create today, the community that once created the Sacred Scriptures? Our potentials are greater than we know.

In particular, it is right to ask whether or not the early community under the guidance of the Holy Spirit could have committed itself to certain structures as it committed itself to the Scriptures. Among scholars there is a great deal of discussion about the origin of the institution of the ministerial and cultic priesthood, about the role of bishops, presbyters and deacons. There are renewed attempts, steadily frustrated, to discover an absolutely clear indication from Scripture how these institutions arose and how far they were meant to be permanent. While some sober scholars recognize that we simply do not have enough historical evidence to solve the problem on the basis of scriptural texts only, those more given to hypotheses present us with various constructions built on the early documents. In one way or another, though, uncertainty remains.

This uncertainty is then transposed into our times. It is claimed that since we have no clear solution in the biblical texts, we cannot have much light about our present situation either. The conclusion is drawn that our institutions as they developed are accretions. They are like trees without roots. Not only do they not stand firmly, they also threaten those who come near them. In the practical order the credit of ministerial priesthood is destroyed, or the value of the sacrament is contested. After all, there is no evidence in the Scriptures for them.

But the matter is more complex. If we assume (as we have to) that the early community had a creative capacity *in the Spirit*, could it have not created new structures — as it created the Scriptures? The main question then would not be what is in the text of the Scriptures, but what did the community *do* even if they did not put it into writing. This position is not as absurd as it looks. Why should the creativity of the community be restricted to writing? Why could not they create new forms of life or specific ways of santification?

We can go even further and ask why the community could not have a creative capacity today? If the creation of structures by the early community was possible, could the community of today create new ones or substantially change some of the old ones? Granted, the Scriptures could not be subject to such reform. But could the institutions? The answer seems to be that in some cases at least the community recognized the action of the Spirit and received structures developed in early times as permanent—much in the same way that the Scriptures are permanent. The ratification of a structure by an ecumenical council (or by councils) would be precisely a sign of such recognition. In some other cases the community certainly did not commit itself strongly to an institution. Then a change, even a radical change, is possible.

The relationship between the community and the Scriptures is complex. The primacy in the process was on the side of the community: the Scriptures were created by it. Yet the Scriptures have become a guiding norm for the community, *they* assumed a new primacy, permanent and immutable. No one can abolish them. But with the living Spirit the community still creates new and unexpected insights into the old writings.

Was the creative capacity restricted to Scriptures — or was it extended also to produce structures? If it was, do we have with structures a phenomenon similar to that of the Scriptures; do we have permanent and unchangeable structures? In some cases, in particular in the cases of the primacy, episcopacy, and ministerial priesthood, there are signs of a permanent creation: the ecumenical councils vouchsafe for the substance of these institutions, they witness the ever permanent and ever developing faith of the Church. But even permanent structures would be subject to new insights and understandings — no less than the text of the Scriptures. A broad field for development!

Among all these puzzling questions a practical rule emerges strong and clear: simplistic solutions to complex problems are no solutions at all, however seriously they are proposed or however strongly they refer to biblical texts or the lack of them. Deep-lying fundamental issues are still to be clarified. We are learning the mysteries of the Kingdom and we are more at the threshold of knowledge than right in the center of it. Yet it is good to know that in all this process the Spirit of God holds the community together and takes care of its progress.

THE CHURCH IN
2001 A.D.

Mankind is progressing by leaps and bounds. Not only do we build up a new world around us with the help of science and intelligence, but our horizons expand. Through our rockets we have a tiny chink to look into the immensity of space. Through our search into the deep regions of the earth we discover the past. There remains one baffling challenge though: the future. What to do about it: we cannot accept defeat! To show that we are knowledgeable we make predictions based on calculations, we nurse expectations grounded on our desire. Happen what may, we do not want the future to elude us.

If we do not know what is to come, let fancy fly. It does, undaunted, in books, articles and speeches. Christians, too, join the great movement of exploration. One of their popular questions is: what does the future hold for the Church? If we just knew that the Church will withstand the battering of new times, we would have more security and we could dedicate ourselves *really*, *hopefully* to the service of the Christian community. To the contrary, if the reasonable expectation is that the Church will not survive, we can leave it in good time.

Understandably, any prediction for the future is welcome. To ground our service in future security is in our blood.

Solemn-faced theologians bent on theories and sociologists waving their questionnaires come to our rescue and shower us with facts and opinions that reveal future development. Their efforts are noble but they are grounded on what is conceivable and predictable. But you cannot speak about the future of the Church without taking into account the inconceivable and unpredictable: the work of God's Spirit who is present with the chosen people, that is, with the whole family of mankind. He has a tender care and compassionate love for *all* with no distinction of nationality, creed, race, sex, or anything at all. The Christian community is one of his instruments to reveal and to spread the Word of God and the love of God to all creatures. We can more or less foresee and foretell what man will do between now and 2001 A.D. We have no insight into what the Spirit will do during the same years.

The Church in 2001 A.D.

True, Christianity is a future-oriented religion. The community waits for the coming of Christ. The prayer, *Maranatha — Come, O Lord Jesus!* — began early and has never ceased to be repeated for so many centuries. Yet, strangely enough the Lord did not reveal much of the immediate future of his people. Some basic facts were enough: the Church will stand; the Word of God will not perish; the fire of the Spirit will not be extinguished. Apart from these fundamental promises very little else was said about the future by the Lord of all ages.

Jesus' message is that the best way to build a Church of the future is to concentrate on the task of the present. We are pilgrims who know where we come from, who may know also where we stand now, but we do not have much idea about the precise goal of our pilgrimage or the exact road leading to it.

It is not given to us to know the Church of 2001 A.D. We can take good-humoredly the foresight of theologians and the calculations of sociologists once we know how limited their knowledge is bound to be. In our heart we can accept a more serious challenge: to go on our pilgrim way into the unknown from one place to another, from joy to sorrow and from tears to laughter. Our security does not spring from the knowledge of the future, but from the help that we experience at present. Our future is hidden, but who worries? The present tasks are immense.

MEANINGFUL LITURGY

In the wake of Vatican Council II a great movement started for meaningful liturgy. A few years ago this movement looked like a small brook, fast, clear and fresh, but confined between narrow borders. Today it looks more like a mighty river, flowing through inland regions and bringing life to what before was a desert. God has not forgotten his people; we have new prayers, new songs and new feasts: *alleluia*. Admittedly, there are discordant voices in the community but by and large the people of God respond to the new initiatives with an ever-more resounding *amen*. Our churches, our homes and even the fields and forests, the valleys and mountains resound with the celebration of pilgrims.

Pilgrims as we are, we should not be walking all the time. Neither should we be incessantly celebrating. Undue frequency should not take away the taste of the feast. Singing beyond measure should not kill the joy. Good pilgrims know that there is time for marching and there is time for resting. There is time for chanting and there is time for listening to inner voices.

In one of the quiet moments let us reflect what is really a *meaningful liturgy*.

Liturgy has many definitions. None of them complete; many of them good enough to contribute to a fuller understanding. One character in the definitions stands out. Liturgy contains visible signs of God's invisible covenant with his people. The signs are not miracles; they are ordinary things and events in the extraordinary context of religious celebration. In the assembly of the faithful simple human words and gestures, the acts of washing and anointing, promises given and taken, a simple meal of bread and wine become saving events of eternal significance. Under the cover of material things divine strength works for our salvation — a thought frequent in earlier Christian centuries.

Meaningful liturgy is, then, the wholeness of signs: the signs have a meaning and they communicate it. To have such wholeness we feel baptism should be real *washing*: the old man should be buried in the water so that the new man could rise out of it. A symbolism that St. Paul very much appreciated. The old baptistries in Rome were constructed exactly for that. Further, bread consecrated at the Eucharist should be *bread* and not some thin wafer that no person could call food. There is no problem about wine. We did not succeed in spoiling its natural form. But the meal again should be a meal; the whole community should share God's table. For the other sacraments, too, as for any celebration, we want strong and clear signs to lift up the mind and heart.

Experience already confirms that wherever a more meaningful liturgy has been introduced the community experiences new strength.

Yet, as with all movements, there comes a point of disillusionment. We hear already that liturgy is not enough. It certainly does not bring us the eschatological Kingdom with all its promises fulfilled. Moreover, the initiatives in liturgy seem to be limited; creativity in many places has run its course. Yet the drive for meaningful liturgy cannot be over!

To see clearer in the dilemma that is very real today let us call to mind what the signs in liturgy are expected to accomplish. They are there, above all, to impress on us the presence of a mystery. They are there to lead us into the ineffable presence of God. Their main purpose is *not* to keep our attention long: we are on our way to *a person*, no thing or ceremony, however sacred it may be, can satisfy our deepest desires. A meaningful sign is not the one that gives full understanding: our aim is union with a person. We have to go beyond all signs.

Meaningful liturgy, therefore, is not the one that tires out the community by an infinity of new forms that the mind and heart cannot restfully receive and assimilate. Neither is meaningful liturgy the one that delights with excitement beyond measure and captivates the pilgrim in his progress to a person. Meaningful liturgy, rather, is the one that is composed of delightfully intelligent signs which communicate a sense of mystery.

To educate our people toward a better participation in liturgy is to awake in them through all signs, ancient and new, the experience of God present. All human words and gestures, signs and symbols are limited. There comes a point, and often it comes soon, when they have fulfilled their purpose: the pilgrims are in the presence of mystery.

Admittedly, we have reflected merely on one aspect of liturgy. Signs are important: without them we could not walk to our destination. The most meaningful signs are those that lead us best beyond all signs: into the mysterious presence of our God among his people. A presence no sign can describe.

ECUMENICAL WORK

It is difficult to find a good analogy to describe those who are working for the unity of Christian churches. At times they are called bridge-builders. There is some truth in the image. They try to build a bond, a link among those who have drifted apart. Yet the unity they are seeking to create is greater than any bridge can achieve. After all, the two shores remain far apart. There is just a narrow passage connecting them: the bridge. We want a greater unity than a bridge can achieve between distant shores. At times they are called ambassadors of peace since their task is to keep dialogue open among divided brethren. Yet ambassadors do not unite different nations. They rather accentuate the division. We want more than distinct kingdoms in intense conversation. We want unity that is real, vital, penetrating, yet not absorbing differences. Indeed, it is not lands and nations that are divided; Christianity is broken. And it has to be welded together.

To weld together two pieces of metal so that they should become one is a difficult art. It is done through fire. A good description of the one who works for the unity of Christian churches is that he stands in the middle of this welding process. He feels the burning fire in his flesh and bones. No person should be in such a position unless he is rich in love in every direction, a source of love for both sides he wants to unite. Through him the broken pieces should become one and regain their original strength.

The work has its own exigencies; to carry it out a deep conversion of mind and heart is necessary. This is the reason why no one can become a good ecumenist overnight. Thank God, we have many good ecumenists coming from both sides who are ready for the sacrifice and do much to heal the break. But, as always happens, there are false prophets around. The ratifying sign that some-one has received the grace to work for this unity is that his love expands in every direction: to Catholics, Lutherans, Calvinists, without distinc-tion because love is not based on any creed or on membership in any community. True love is there because there is a rich source, not because there is a discriminate taste in choosing the object. If some-one loves in one direction but not in the other he is not a builder of unity. To become a true ecumenist means to extend the limits of love and understand-ing; what embraced earlier one Christian community embraces them all now. Catholics as well as Protestants can go through external change without conversion of heart. They can simply shift the object of their loyalty without expanding their charity. Catholics who suddenly begin to love all things Protestant but have no compassion for the wounds and sufferings of their own church are not ecumenists. They are as small in their charity as they were before. To caricature the pope or the bishops shows as little love as to mock the head and the elders of a Protestant communion. The same would be true of a Protestant, if ecumenism for him meant to be friendly with Catholics and neglect his own community. There is no substitute for real love. When it is missing it betrays itself.

No one can be an ecumenist who hates his own family. To work for the unity of the churches is to be a source of love and compassion in all directions.

PRAYER AND DANCING

We conceived prayer too much as a little speech given by man to God. Then we analyzed and classified it. The speech could be a prayer of *petition* for a thing we needed, or it could *give thanks* for benefits received. It could be a prayer of *praise*, pure worship given to God. But prayer had to be a speech from man to God.

No wonder so many good Christians grew tired of prayer. After all, they had to listen to their own clumsy words, even if directed to God. The desire of their hearts is greater than words can express. It soars beyond human speech right to the ineffable. St. Augustine was right: we have been created for God and our heart remains restless till we find him.

If one could only cancel out all the false definitions and prejudices about prayer the situation would improve immediately: there would be more Christians who pray. Prayer is not man talking to God but God talking to man. All begins by God's graceful initiative. We can only respond.

Right there is the clue to good prayer: a capacity to listen to God. He does not use clumsy little words to communicate with us. We are immersed in him more than the fish is immersed in the ocean or the birds are at home in the air. He is in our innermost being. He is in the depths of our heart that we ourselves cannot reach. Some understanding of this closeness of God to us is necessary to perceive his communications. His presence in us is like quiet light that gives understanding. His presence is a source of power that gives strength. He reaches out to the whole person. He attracts our mind to truth. He increases our sensitivity to beauty. He infuses quiet strength when it is necessary to carry the burden of the day.

To pray is to respond to God with our mind and heart, our body and soul, our flesh and spirit, with our whole person. The best image of this life of response is a man and woman dancing together in perfect rhythm. The man leads the woman through the most complex of movements and she responds so well that for an outsider it is near impossible to see where the prompting comes from. Yet the man has the initiative and communicates it in many subtle ways.

God's communications too are subtle and gentle; they cannot be put into words. They have a mysterious character. Man's response should be similar: subtle and gentle, engaging the whole person.

In fact, when we look at the whole extent of the

relationship between God and man, we understand why no verbal communication can really do justice to it. Words express a small part, and a very small part only, of a great friendship. Indeed, it is not enough to repeat the words, *Lord, Lord*; we have to respond with our whole person in action. Those who do not dance with the Lord in this world (he leading) will have no share in his Kingdom.

Some consequences emerge to help us pray well.

First of all, the words we speak have only a relative importance, although they are not superfluous. Words have the power to warm up our humanity to the perception of God's initiative and to a good response to it. This warming-up process is the purpose of any good reading of the Scriptures, of any devoted meditation on the great events of our redemption. They build up a sensitivity in us to notice the subtle voice of the Spirit and to respond to it. A tuning-up process for better things.

Then, it follows that one can pray well without words, just by receiving light and strength when the mind and heart are at rest. A receptivity has to be there, certainly; an attentive attitude, a freedom to listen. God frequently communicates understanding and strong love without words. When he does we can assimilate them without much effort — or any effort at all. Not an extraordinary state. After all, none of us can give grace to himself; we can only receive it. To pray in this receptive way is like sitting by the fire and receiving its warmth. The fire is there, our body and soul absorb the heat without thinking of it or even wanting it. The effect of it all becomes manifest when one goes out into the cold. The comforting warmth remains with us in our body for a long time.

One should not be afraid of thinking nothing and doing nothing when God is giving plenty. The action is there but from the part of the Spirit. To pray well can mean to absorb quiet strength.

Finally, it is clear that good prayer does not take anyone away from action. It is the source of action. To give time for a meal is not leaving the work behind. It is to store up energy for the work. There is no greater nonsense than to believe that depth can be reached in Christian life, and energy can be accumulated for action without peaceful recollection in God. Such concentration takes time, of course. Good and nourishing meals always take time; athletes cannot live on snacks. From recollection, action will always follow because man has to respond to God with his whole person, and creative action is an integral part of man's life. Moreover, God is most concerned about the world — to the point of action: he has given his Son for it. Therefore, he will inspire those who listen to him to action that consists in giving.

Verbal prayer is really a small part in the wholeness of Christian life. It is the beginning of a response that must expand to our whole being. The response has to be total. In a dance whose beauty transcends our desire and imagination God is the leading partner. We have to respond with our words, our eyes, our limbs, our whole body. This analogy is at home in all religions: man always incorporated sacred dancing into his worship. In our modern liturgy the responses in which our whole body takes part are reduced to bows and genuflections. There is room and need for some better movements in our sanctuaries to symbolize that God is our leading partner in a sacred dance that he initiated.

I BELIEVE IN GOD'S
UNHOLY CHURCH

Strange title! How can anyone believe in an unholy Church when the sign of God's presence among us is precisely holiness, and the Church should be the first to be marked by it? Besides, such a new profession of faith in an unholy Church is against the canons of the Third Council of Constantinople (A.D. 681), which forbade the composition of any new Creed. Yet every generation of Christians should have their own profession of faith, which proclaims the permanent Christian message but stresses the truths most important for them.

Today we need to profess our faith in God's unholy Church. To accept this unholiness in our midst is far more difficult than to believe in the existence of an immaculate community shining with virtue and goodness. This is the problem of our times.

There is no other Church than an unholy Church. True, there are divine gifts in the Church, and there is holiness, too, in plenty. The People of God are assisted by the Spirit of God more than the Hebrews fleeing from Egypt and wandering in the desert were ever assisted. True, the children of God are all clothed by immortality, and their community is destined to be everlasting. Yet precisely the same people are a community of sinners. They are sanctified, yes, but they carry their gifts in fragile vases; they are healed but they are not glorified. The joy of the redemption is in their hearts; yet the same hearts remain human with the burden of limitation, shortcoming, narrowness and sin.

We are all in need of mercy and understanding.

This sinful quality of the members extends all over the Church. No one is exempted. It affects young and old, men and women; it is not deleted by dignity, rank or education. It is not taken away when a member is consecrated to minister the Word and the sacraments to his brethren; bishops and priests remain sinners, too.

Yet for a Christian every sin is a lucky event, the *felix culpa*: the sin of man brings us God's goodness. We can enjoy his mercy, and precisely because all are sinners in the Church we can feel ourselves at home in it. We can feel that we belong to it, we can relax in it. What human being would not be embarrassed and ill at ease in a community of glorious saints? And, of course, our priests and bishops share the common condition.

Admittedly, the grace of God breaks through the human surface. The Holy Spirit is keeping the Word of God alive in the Church. He leads the hesitant pilgrims to the Kingdom. But while we are on the way, human limitations and sinfulness are manifest at all levels. It simply cannot be any other way. Our Church, praise be to God, *is* a human Church. Those who hold a public office are more exposed than others and their limitations are more evident even if they have less of them. Their responsibility is great.

Our response to such a human Church can be only that of love — love that has learned to give and is not eager to take. When the traveler between Jerusalem and Jericho was robbed and beaten up so that he was bleeding from his wounds, the priest and the Levite passed him by. They may have been intent on the splendor of the Law and did not notice the bleeding human being. The Samaritan, the lowly man, understood the situation and showed his love in deeds. When the Pilgrim Church shows its wounds, and its strength is bleeding away — be it for past neglect, be it for present narrowness, be it for lack of foresight for the future — there is one response only that springs from evangelical love: to help and to heal. To pass by, discoursing on a holiness that should be in the community, is not a sign of love.

To believe in God's Church as far as it is holy,

immaculate, wise and sinless is to indulge in an overspiritualized dream and to reject the humanity of our God who delights himself in our sinful company.

One day (the Bible calls it the Day of the Lord), holiness will take the place of all sinfulness, and the glory of the children of God will be manifest. Meanwhile, we can relax as full-time and full-fledged members of a sinful community where each helps to carry the other's burden.

FOR CONSCIENCE'S SAKE

Our age is often described as an age of technology with a loss of humanity. Nothing could be further from the truth. Granted there are advances in technology, but side by side there *is* progress in humanity. True, computers are taking over much of the work of our brains, but man has not become the slave of machines. One sign of his increasing freedom is a respect for the human person, which is emerging with a strength unheard of in past history. In particular, there is an insistence on acknowledging the right of each man to follow his conscience.

This trend is so strong that even totalitarian states find it necessary for gaining international good will to insert into their constitution the right of every citizen to freedom of conscience. It is a cynical attitude, since pious theory is not followed by honest practice; yet there is a ray of hope even there. Freedom *is* affirmed in the constitution: a true and good vision. Given enough time the citizens will ask for its implementation. Man was born free and free he will be. The ancient Romans knew that nothing can prevail against nature. *Chase nature out with a pitchfork*, they said, *and it will return*. There is a movement all over the earth, however weak it may be in some places, to give its due to our humanity.

The movement is fostered by many psychologists, philosophers and theologians who for once go hand-in-hand to affirm the right of a person to follow his conscience. They all say that each person must be true to his own light. If not, a dangerous split is introduced into his life. No one should be constrained to act against his moral judgment and no one should be impeded from acting according to it — unless his action would be against the well-being of the community.

The psychologist grounds his argument on the need for *wholeness* in the person, or on the need for harmony between vision and action. The philosopher speaks about the dignity of a human person and his inviolable right to be himself. The theologian adds a particular firmness to his colleague's conclusion when he affirms that the rule of conscience is so absolute that God himself judges man accordingly.

An age that achieves such a good development has nothing to fear. Progress in technology did not destroy humanity.

Yet with all this exaltation of conscience, there

is a critical question. What *is* conscience? All speak about it, few venture to define it. All have some insight into it, no one fathoms it.

Naturally enough, our contribution will be limited too. It will simply speak about the absolute and relative aspects that are present together in every judgment of conscience.

Let us begin by saying what conscience is not. Negations may lead to affirmations. Conscience is not a blind and irrational force. If it were, it would destroy the dignity of man. To subject a person to a categorical imperative that has no rhyme or reason behind it is to deny his rationality — that is, his humanity. A blind force to be obeyed slavishly destroys freedom; the more so when the force is from the inside. It takes away the right to assess and judge ourselves and our actions critically.

Neither is conscience a set of static rules imprinted into our minds as the Commandments were carved into stones. Conscience is a dimension of a living, growing, developing man. Everything moves inside him; his mind and heart change and grow every day in wisdom and grace. A static conscience would mean a dead man — who has no conscience.

Nor is conscience an agent independent from the external world and from the community that surrounds a person. It is rather a force that compels a person to integrate with the outside world and community. If conscience were an autonomous agent intent on the good of one man, it would produce monsters, unfit to live and walk among us.

If conscience is not a blind force, not a set of static rules, not a ruler independent from the outside world, what is it then?

By the rule of opposites, we should say that conscience is a capacity to form intelligent judgments, a capacity that grows and develops, and eventually leads us to harmonious integration with the world and our fellow men.

Conscience is concerned with intelligent judgments about our practical attitudes and actions. There is a fundamental thrust in man to go forward, to fulfil himself and to find his place in the universe. At every moment of his progress he has to form a judgment and make a decision about the next step. Intelligence and critical talent have a lot to do with their correctness. When someone does not have anything better than an erroneous, or worse still, a stupid judgment, he has to follow it since he has nothing else to follow. Moreover, respect is due to him; after all, everyone is entitled to make mistakes within reasonable bounds. We must grant freedom to a sincere man of bad judgment. God himself respects our limitations and such persons will probably make up much of the population in heaven.

Conscience is an ever-growing and developing capacity. It shares in the dynamic character of man. It progresses from childish simplicity to wisdom seasoned by age and experience. It is never perfect because there is always more to be absorbed and to be understood. It never stops in its drive toward a better decision. Yet, all this mobility does not exclude stability: fundamental inspirations and visions remain identical while they expand. After all, the identity of a person does not change while he explores the unknown and is enriched by new discoveries. When a conscience stops growing, the best portion of man begins to die. A static conscience is hardly better than a computer that churns out the same solutions all over again. Yet, yet — here is the mystery: a computer-like conscience is to be respected — because a man is worthy of respect even when he is a dwarf. But do not sing the praise of dwarfness; it is an affliction crying out for help and medication.

Conscience should lead a person to integration with the world outside him. Such integration is possible because of the complex nature of conscience. Its judgment is brought about through the delicate play of an internal thrust and the impressions gathered from outside. They, together lead to knowledge, understanding and a critically grounded decision. Through well-made practical judgments man finds his place in the universe.

When a little fellow is born his consciousness is centered on his physical well-being: a primitive manifestation of human life. As his intelligence unfolds he begins to understand the need of integrating himself into the world outside of him. Gradually he learns the moral imperative of rules, precepts, and commands. He realizes that without accepting them he cannot be incorporated into a human community, in practice, into his family.

A mysterious force operates in every man, a force that pushes him to go out of himself. It makes him realize the need for help and support from others and makes him accept his duty to contribute to the welfare of others.

The process of integration is a delicate art, an on-going event. It is never achieved; every moment brings new knowledge of the world and a new understanding of oneself. Therefore, anyone who relies on a judgment of conscience that is not the fruit of integration is like a driver who plans his course in disregard of the highways. He can do untold damage — to himself and to all who are unlucky enough to meet him on his crazy course. Yet as long as the public menace has not materialized, the light of the person, limited as it is, has to be respected — and watched with utmost care. With all due respect, barricades must be built. Such precautionary manuevers are highly sensitive. Although the driver is entitled to our respect since he is our fellow man, his way of driving should not serve as a model to any man.

All this told, the conclusion emerges: in every sincere judgment of conscience there is something *absolute*, commanding respect from God and man, and there is something *relative*, crying out for ever-increasing maturity. Every judgment of conscience perfects man and brings out his imperfection. All in one act; all at the same time.

Therefore, the wise man who is faithful to his conscience can make a firm stand or can retrace his steps to correct his path if necessary. In any case, even when he makes a firm stand he anticipates the joy of walking again to discover new vistas for ever better stands.

A THEOLOGICAL
MEDITATION ON
OBEDIENCE

To speak about the theological concept of obedience is to conjure up practical problems. The questions that jump into our minds are how Christian peoples have to obey the pope, diocesan priests their bishop, or religious their superior. Or, again, how the faithful in the parish should or should not obey their pastor. Yet, the answer to the problem of obedience is found not so much in pragmatic solutions of difficult cases but in theological reflections. Vision is necessary before action.

The data for these reflections have to come from theological sources. It would be tempting to enumerate them in the conventional order: the witnessing of the Scriptures, the Fathers, the prayer life of the community, the practice of saints, and so on.

But it is insufficient. Today we are groping toward some new sources: the *sensus fidelium*, the signs of the times, the *consensus* of mankind on some important issues, the insights of non-Catholic Christians, and others. Moreover, the hermeneutical problem has descended on us and we are healthily confused about the use of all sources old and new.

The Church itself, that is, the community with its complex and organic structure is the best hermeneutical principle: the community has to weigh the importance of the sources. But before a final conclusion is reached there is a long process through doubts and hesitations. Theology itself has become a pilgrim wandering through a certain darkness — we are not sure if it is the twilight before the night or the dawn of a new day.

Our theological conclusions about obedience too will suffer from uncertainties in the premises. This state of theology reflects the natural condition of the Church. Christ himself did not give absolute clarity to his disciples. He helped them onto the road to the Father. He promised to give them enough light for the duration of their pilgrimage. The early Church in fact had some fundamental certainties and many uncertainties. This primitive condition we have regained today. We experience both the certainty of faith and the uncertainty of our reflections.

Obedience used to be a simple concept, the submission of a person to another person. There were different degrees in the submission but not much variety in the definition.

Now we are in search of a better understanding of obedience; the old definition is questioned.

* * * * *

Before we can formulate a new theology of obedience we have to find out the causes of our present confusion or ignorance. Here are two of them:

(a) Obedience is response to authority. Therefore, our understanding of obedience hinges on our conception of authority. Today we are discussing and investigating new dimensions in authority. Since we are confused about authority we are confused about obedience also.

(b) Authority is but one manifestation of the life of the community. But our understanding of community in general, and of the Christian community in particular has undergone a rapid development in the last decade without achieving final clarity. Consequently, because we are confused about community, we are confused about authority as well.

In other words, to reach a better understanding of obedience we need a new vision of *authority* since obedience and authority always go together. They are related to each other like the call and the answer are related. Incidentally, it is not always easy to determine which side calls and which responds, especially in person-to-person relationships. There is always a complex exchange of calls and answers coming from both sides.

Further we discover that we need a deeper realization of the meaning of *community* because the authority-obedience relationship functions in a community. The exchange between the one-who-calls (head) and the one-who-responds (member) can be understood only within a community, that is always an organic unity — otherwise there is simply no community. When searching for the meaning of obedience we are exploring a relationship between two persons. Since they are intelligent and blessed with free will—a creative capacity—the relationship is *sui generis*; it is among persons. But the issue does not stop there, it is more complex because God enters the scene; his sovereign action inspires both those in authority and those who obey. All share something of the power of God in different ways.

The main point is that one cannot theologize about obedience in itself. We have to retrace our steps to more fundamental realities.

Precisely because the development of our thought about community and authority has not advanced enough we cannot give a final answer to obedience. We are in the middle of a search, not in a process of consolidation or conclusion.

Yet there is one permanent element in obedience. Obedience is a personal attitude. It is a virtue in the classical sense of being an act *(actus)* or an ingrained habit *(habitus)*. It is the orientation of a person, the orientation being the result of an option to submit oneself to an authority in community.

Obedience, then, is a disposition of persons towards each other. It is a manifestation of life in community. All the different dimensions of a Christian community are there: the relationship between God and the group, God and an individual human person, and also the relationship between one member and another.

It is in this personal context that we can understand that obedience is really a particular aspect of communion, love between persons.

* * * * *

Obedience can certainly mean a person-to-person relationship between God and man, an absolute relationship, in the sense that man owes absolute obedience to God. Yet, it is not absolute in the sense that God wants to destroy the work of his hands (the intelligence and freedom of man) through obedience. He wants man to be his own image: creative in his freedom.

This intention of God is rarely taken into account. The dependence of man on God is stressed, but not the intention of God to raise man to a level of equality. Therefore, we get a distorted idea of obedience because we do not see it in the dynamics of love that postulates equality.

In fact, from the beginning of our salvation history, obedience to God appears as absolute and relative at the same time. True, man owes complete obedience to God. Yet God is seeking a partnership, a friendship, a love relationship of which the most tender symbolic expressions are in the Canticle of Canticles. Since those songs have been written and incorporated into the inspired revelation of God there is no other perfect image of obedience than that exuberant, overflowing celebration of the love-relationship that is described in them. The Law, including the Ten Commandments, and so many ritual prescriptions are simply a preparation for it. We are now touching on the covenant relationship where man, small and dependent as he is, is raised to a near-equal partnership with God.

In the New Testament the process is completed when Christ tells his disciples at the Last Supper that they are not servants anymore; they are friends. This friendship includes the sharing of Jesus' life, of his sufferings and of his joy in the resurrection.

We understand, then, why a merely legal obedience, not integrated into love or not developed into this exuberant love relationship, remains frustrating for a Christian.

Real Christian relationship is dynamic, it is a process and it takes a long time to develop. The relationship of obedience toward God that matures into love is the prototype for obedience among men which, too, has to be integrated into a love relationship.

The process, therefore, in which obedience develops is part of a movement initiated by God who tries to make man equal to himself. That is the lesson of the Incarnation: it is not only that God was made man, but that man shares the nature and the life of God. The purpose of obedience is to lead man to this equality. Therefore, the authority and obedience relationship is not valid within the Christian context unless those who have authority try to make those who have to obey equal to themselves.

* * * * *

Obedience, however, has a communitarian dimension too. It can be conceived as a dedication of a person to the community. Since Christian community has a specific value in itself, such dedication is justified.

We really cannot live without a community; community is an essential life element for all of us. We need it as fish need water to live or birds need air to fly. Without community our life is truncated and our development is paralyzed. This need is a fundamental human necessity, instituted and respected by God himself. Historically he first spoke to a community, the Hebrew tribes, the heirs of Yahweh's promises. Jesus himself founded a community. From the beginning to follow him meant dedication to the building of a new community.

At this point we have reached the heart of the matter; the understanding of the Christian community of faith and love is the clue to the understanding of authority and consequently of obedience.

The Christian community comes into being through the inspiration of the Spirit of God and it is cemented together by the Word of God. All members of the community owe obedience to the Spirit and the Word. The fruit of this obedience is the community.

Yet this is not all. In the community the same divine intention and force operate that brought about the Incarnation — the coming of God into this world to heal, redeem, and sanctify all men. The dedication of Christ to man is alive in the Christian community; the community should be dedicated to man.

If the obedience of the individual member is dedication to the community, the community of believers has to obey the community of man. The affirmation is true although paradoxical and in need of some qualifications.

The Church is in possession of the Good News brought us by Christ. In presenting the Good News to the world the Church has to obey the signs of the times existing outside of the Christian community. Such signs are: the specific needs of man at a given age or at a particular place; the patterns of thought and life of divers peoples and nations; the great events of history. Such accommodation in communication and service is the *kenosis* of the Church, it is truly obedience to the world. Obviously, it is rooted in obedience to the Spirit and the Word.

This *kenosis* is a moral duty for the Church. As Christ did not grasp the glory that was due to him but rather emptied himself for the sake of man, so the Christian community should and must do the same. Through such obedience the Church becomes a mediator; God and the human family are cemented together.

* * * * *

Obedience for the individual member in the community means fidelity to the community itself. A covenant arises between a member and the whole Christian community. One takes care of the other, a kind of shared responsibility, although the word is too juridical. It is really an abundance of charity toward each other, with a willingness to give in an unlimited measure.

This supposes an openness in which the needs of one are known and the others obey the call to help. Therefore, the first to obey are the ones who preside. The solemn papal title, Servant of the Servants of God, is not just a meaningless decoration but, if it is taken seriously, the blunt expression of a theological reality. The pope is the first who has to obey the call to heal, to redeem and to sanctify all the members. The same obedience binds the bishops and the presbyters toward their people. The rest of the faithful are not dispensed from obedience since they too have to minister to the needs of the servants, the pope, the bishops and the priests.

This obedience again operates in balance with obedience to the Spirit and to the Word of God. Obviously, it can exist only in the context of the Gospel. But even so, it exists *in a human community* where all things are imperfect. Laws and precepts are all marked with imperfection, sometimes to a high degree. These human limitations produce many problems and tensions.

The answer to the problems is in the great value of the substantial unity of the community. It is so reasonable to remain one that for the sake of it some unreasonableness can be tolerated. Tensions will follow. But they are necessary to carry the community forward, they are moving forces. To eliminate them could bring paralysis.

Therefore, I am not even sure if it would be good for the community to have a clear idea of authority and obedience. To search for the right idea through partial insights moves the community in the right direction.

*   *   *   *   *

This concept of obedience is rooted in a vision of the Church that cannot be stressed enough today. The Church, that is *a community*, is a sign inserted by God into our human history. It was, it is and it will be an ambivalent sign. It is marked by God's grace, but it carries the traces of our sins too. Because of this ambivalent character, balance and understanding are required in the person who reads the sign. Some see God's action *only* in it and they misrepresent the reality of the Church when they speak about it. Others will see the vestiges of sinfulness *only* and they falsely conclude that such a community cannot be a sign from God.

Yet, the community is a sign in the sense that it proclaims our redemption *in actu*, in its process of operation, a healing, redeeming and sanctifying process. Therefore, grace and sin are visible and have to be visible at the same time.

In other terms, the Church is not simply the sign of God's holiness. It is not simply the manifestation of our sins and limitations. It is a visible demonstration of grace meeting sin. The sign itself is a paradox and it can be understood only by those who have some understanding of both the mercy of God and the sinfulness of man and how the two need each other.

If obedience is dedication to the community then it is really an act or attitude to build, to uphold the sign that God planted in our history. That is, obedience is a declaration of faith in the visible, tangible, human, holy and sinful Church, in a community in transformation. Obedience is a profession of faith in the visible Church, not perfect, but visibly moving from sin to goodness.

While the biblical concept of *kenosis* is correct and remains valid all through the centuries, there is no doubt that the forms of ecclesiastical obedience were conditioned by the circumstances of time and space and by the theology of the time. A lack of understanding of the organic nature of the Church led to a unilateral conception of obedience. Its communitarian dimensions were lost sight of and it was described as 'accepting the will of another person.' This conception was incomplete and therefore incorrect.

Where does all this lead us? Certainly not to a well defined idea of obedience. Certainly not to an over-all clarity. But, rather, toward an attitude that seeks a union with God through the unity of a human community. Obedience, then, is a disposition that leads a person to uphold the existence and development of Christian community. It springs from an act of faith that the visible Church, sinful and holy as it is, remains one of God's mighty deeds in history.

* * * * *

Some practical conclusions are in order now. The main principle stands, in its clarity and obscurity: obedience is the building up of, the accepting of the unity of the Christian community and the healing of the same unity if it has been broken.

In the practical order, obedience is due primarily to the Holy Spirit and to his commands, directions, inspirations as they reach us.

They mostly do reach us in the Scriptures and through the Christian community. Obedience in faith is due when the whole community or the legitimate organs of authority in the Church with the charism of fidelity declare that some teaching, some fact is part of God's revelation and it is an integral and essential part of our faith.

When the Christian community and the rightful organs of authority are searching for light no one can truly give an assent in faith to a final result that is not known with the certainty of faith at this time. He can give his assent to a process, to a progress. He has to commit himself toward a search for building a unity, which may mean in practice the clarification of a doctrinal point.

Obedience to human laws has to be based on theological principles. No one except God has authority over his children. If the community has any authority it is only because it was given by God. Therefore, any human law has to be interpreted in a much broader context of obeying God.

Any kind of merely legal obedience in a Christian context is always frustrating and in fact destroys Christian life because law cannot redeem anyone. Either there is a dynamic strength in obedience developing into love or it is really not Christian obedience at all.

INFALLIBILITY

REVISITED

The ecumenical dialogue among theologians succeeds when no one of the parties is entrenched in
his own position trying to explain to the other what
he thinks; it succeeds when all parties are one in
contemplating God's mysteries. When they eye
each other, arguing and gesticulating, there is no
communication; when they look together at God
and his deeds among men there is no division.
From that moment, conquering attitudes and de-
fensive battles vanish; the condition for the right
way of theologizing is established.

Plato said with much truth that a philosopher is
born when a pe son looking at our universe and all
the things in it experiences *pathos*, a certain anxiety
in face of the unknown. A similar idea is present in

the Christian tradition. A theologian is born when a person experiences wonder and admiration in the presence of God's mysteries.

Frankly, there is plenty of wonder and little admiration for the infallibility that Vatican I attributed to the pope. Of course, it was shown soon after the Council, and it has been ever since, that the conditions for the operation of this charism are stringent, and not all ordinary pronouncements of the pope are guaranteed by the Holy Spirit. Rather, in most of the pope's statements the proclamation of the Word of God is mixed with human wisdom and knowledge. Further, Vatican II opened our eyes to a new dimension about infallibility when it stressed the collegial character of the episcopal body of which the pope is head.

Yet the stumbling block remains. At ecumenical encounters the problem of infallibility, for the most part, is politely avoided. As a consequence the difficulty secretly lingers on and nothing is solved. Unity is not increasing.

Admittedly, the term infallibility sounds all-embracing. It is negative and does not convey its own limitations. Also, because it is negative, it does not really say what infallibility is. We have to look behind the expression.

Is it possible that the clumsy word "infallibility" covers a mystery of which Vatican I had a glimpse but did not have either the time or the means to make explicit? Could we Christians of today investigate and, if we discover a mystery, contemplate it — together? And increase our unity?

I submit that the mystery behind the doctrine of infallibility as Catholics understand it is the fidelity of God to his people. This fidelity is independent of all human factors. It is the fidelity that God has sworn to Abraham and his descendants — as valid today as it was in the beginning; Paul the apostle pointed this out forcefully to his Galatians. God's fidelity to his people culminated in the physical presence of Christ to us errant and erring children of God. Christ was the Word, and also he gave us the Word, not that it should be lost but that it should shine in the darkness. Through the Gospel he left the Word with us that no man should be deprived of the joy of hearing the Good News. He left us the presence of a quietly strong light.

One particular aspect of Christian faith in which differing communities converge is belief in the fidelity of God, who preserves his Word in the midst of his people, through the vicissitudes of our history. This fidelity is explained in many ways. The acceptance of the Scriptures as a guide for authentic Christian life (so firmly held among Protestants) is a way of expressing belief in the fidelity of God. To this the Orthodox Church adds great reverence toward traditions, for they are convinced that the Word of God cannot be erased by the deeds of men. Catholics go one step further—their faith is that the fidelity of God to his people is manifest and operative through living persons, the sacramentally consecrated bishops, and in particular through the head of their community, the pope. This, Vatican I may not have said well, but Vatican II made much progress in redressing the balance.

Infallibility may be a clumsy term, but it tries to express a wondrous deed: the mysterious and permanent presence of the Word in the Church. How can we say this mystery fully? Was there any time in history when man did not stutter in the presence of God?

All Christian communities without exception believe that God remains faithful to his people, and his Word is not covered up by the dust of centuries but remains alive with a transcendent strength. We did not inherit a corpse from Christ, but a living message. The more or less human instruments of God's fidelity in the eyes of the Protestant are the Holy Scriptures; for the Orthodox they are the Scriptures and traditions and the sacramental episcopate; in the eyes of the Catholic, all of these, but with a special position accorded to the person whom they believe to be the successor of Peter. Behind them all there is the mystery in which we all believe: it is the fidelity of God. We differ in conceiving the manifestation, the channel, the instrument of this faithfulness.

No good comes out of arguments; we have had too many of them. But we can all join together and wonder and marvel at the fact that God is with his people and he keeps his Word alive among them. The experience of this permanent event can be overwhelming. The fascination of mystery and the gratefulness that follows from it can create a unity greater than we ever dared to hope for. This will be one more manifestation of God's fidelity to his people.

DISCERNING THE PRESENCE OF THE HOLY SPIRIT TODAY

The message of Christ to his disciples was good news: a message of freedom. He took the better part of three years to unfold and explain it; then he sealed its authenticity with his death and resurrection. The young Saul who was surprised by the light on his way to Damascus and became Paul grasped the meaning of the message. To this day joy and amazement overflow from his letters to fellow Christians: we are free; we have been freed from the slavery of flesh, of sin, of death. To be a Christian is to be free. To be a Christian is to be a poor pilgrim who has nothing but who possesses all. To be a Christian is not to have treasures on the earth but to possess all the stars; not to have a permanent abode but to have shelter under the wing of God.

But there is no freedom without responsibility. Every charter of freedom is a charter of duties.

To live with freedom requires great wisdom, especially today when the world is more in ferment than ever before. Man is searching to a depth hitherto unknown the secrets of the atom and of the universe. In this search and fermentation the Christian stands sometimes bewildered. New ideas are presented and new ways of life are proposed to him. He wonders how to judge them all, how to distinguish right from wrong.

From the beginning of this search Christians should understand that Christ did not bring to his disciples an immunity from the whirling events of this world and from the subsequent commotion and confusion. On the contrary, he wanted them to be right in the midst of it all. He never promised them a new world order, clear, clean, and antiseptic. Rather, he warned them that their lives would be full of surprises, good and bad, until he comes again. And even his coming is described as the last event of a universal cataclysm where confusion goes to the point that even the stars fall from heaven and the sun and moon are obscured. True, this is symbolic language but it conveys a truth. Christians are not called away from the world. They are called to announce hope, even when the foundations of our universe seem to be shaking.

Christ promised an insecure world to his disciples but gave them the security of a guide. This guide is the Holy Spirit.

Christians believe in the mighty deeds of God among men. The creation of all things is attributed to the immense power of the Father, the redemption of man to the goodness of the Son (he became one of us, Jesus of Nazareth), the sanctification of the world to the strength of the Holy Spirit.

As of old God promised to stay with his people. He kept his promise by sending his Son and when he disappeared from before our eyes he sent the Spirit who is at the source of all good thoughts and all good actions. The Spirit of God is with every man of good will: he guides them towards God's Kingdom. Therefore it is important that we should be able to discern in our heart and in this world the signs of the presence and action of the Holy Spirit so that we could follow him. These few pages are really a new variation on the old theme of the discernment of the action of the Holy Spirit, adapted to new times and new needs. A warning is necessary: no one of the signs we describe is infallible in itself. Several signs must be taken and weighed together, and even so a great deal of wisdom is required to form a balanced judgment.

It is best to begin this exposition with the biblical signs of the presence and action of the Holy Spirit on the day of Pentecost when he was first given to the disciples. These signs are the *wind*, the *fire*, and a *new message in new languages*.

We read in the Acts of the Apostles that on the

143

day of the first Pentecost when the Holy Spirit was given to the Apostles, "Suddenly they heard what sounded like a powerful wind from heaven, the noise of which filled the entire house in which they were sitting" (Acts 2:2). There was a violent wind. *Wind* means a movement of the air; it means a refreshing breeze—and it also means a violent storm that cleans the atmosphere. When the Holy Spirit is present somewhere there is bound to be *a wind* because he is the living God who re-creates the face of the earth. This re-creation of the face of the earth means a great movement which brings fresh air into the life of mankind and of the Church. The wind of Pentecost does not destroy life: it makes the gift of life more abundant — with more movement. If there is no movement at all in a place it is not likely that the Spirit of God, the living God who re-creates the face of the earth, is present there.

We also read in the Acts of the Apostles: "And something appeared to them that seemed like tongues of fire; these separated and came to rest on the head of each of them" (Acts 2:3). *Fire* means dynamism. It means a burning away of the old in order to prepare a place for something new. Whenever the Holy Spirit is present in a person or in an institution he is like fire; he is trying to burn away what is not necessary in order to prepare a place for new gifts which he wants to give. Fire is also the symbol of love — an active love which manifests itself in deeds. We speak about burning love for another person. Such a love will witness the presence of the Spirit.

"They were all filled with the Holy Spirit, and began to speak foreign languages as the Spirit gave them the gift of speech" (Acts 2:4). The *message* the Apostles began to preach was the good news of the resurrection of Christ, and the message was heard in new languages which the Apostles, natives of Galilee, had never spoken before. The person who is working with the Holy Spirit will have a new message; its very newness is a sign of the Spirit. Our Lord said that the Holy Spirit would lead the disciples into all truth. Therefore whoever is blessed by the presence of the Spirit will have new insights into the doctrine of Christ. In consequence he will also preach a new message, the expression of his new insight. He will not simply repeat what he heard from another; he will be able to say something personal. At the same time the new message will be a new insight into an old doctrine — not a destruction but a clarification of our traditions.

From these pentecostal signs we may turn to a classical description of the gifts of the Holy Spirit by St. Paul in his epistle to the Galatians. He writes: "What the Spirit brings is very different: love, joy, peace, patience, kindness, goodness, trustfulness, gentleness and self-control" (Gal 5, 22).

The sign of the presence of the Holy Spirit is *love* in the heart of a good man. Christian love means readiness to give and the measure of love is the extent we give. To give to another our material possessions can be love; but it is merely the beginning of love. The most precious possession we have is our own person and the excess of love begins when someone gives himself to another, not because the other person deserves it but because there is a source of love in the giver that knows no limit. Such love can come only from the Holy Spirit since light and strength from God are necessary to take the risk and to bear the uncertainty that such a giving entails. Not all who claim that they are led by love have this precious gift. But all those who know this excess of giving received a gift from the Holy Spirit even if they never heard of him. It is in love that man becomes the greatest, because love does not know any limitation. Our mind does; our knowledge is always limited. Love begins to soar toward infinity where the finite capacity of our knowledge ends. The sign of the Holy Spirit is to love beyond knowledge.

Joy is another mark of the presence of the Spirit. Not an exuberant emotion that leaves a person exhausted but a happiness that springs from the steady faith in the goodness of all things and of their maker, God. Such joy is compatible with worry, suffering and even agony because the joy is in the depths of the soul and everyday storms cannot disturb it. This joy blossoms out in an optimism, in a faith in the ultimate triumph of what is honest, good, and holy.

The *peace* that the Spirit brings is not the peace of the surface of the lake on a windless day when the gentle and sensitive sailboats float lifelessly on the water. The peace of the Holy Spirit is the quiet trust of those who are in a boat firmly anchored when the storm is raging. Christian peace was never stillness devoid of life, but security on an insecure sea; experiencing all the hazards and difficulties of our exposure to the elements. We have confidence that all things cooperate to the good of those who are loved by God.

The remaining signs, *patience, kindness, goodness, trustfulness, gentleness,* and *self-control* are really a description of love that has learned to give. What should distinguish a Christian is precisely that he has something of the foolishness of God who gives himself to man. Our common sense would suggest to us to calculate, to reserve judgment, not to act until we are fully convinced that we are right. To believe in the ultimate success of foolish love is the mark of the Holy Spirit. No one else can lead a man so far.

To these biblical signs some new principles can be added which may help us to discern the presence and the work of the Holy Spirit. Most of the principles which follow will be based substantially on the same idea. It is this: when in a person, in a doctrine, in an action two extremes are brought together and are united in harmony it is likely that this union is due to the Holy Spirit. Human persons are inclined to exaggerate, to see just one side of two extremes. God is always inclined to create harmony when naturally speaking there would be opposition. This is another way of saying that balance is the most difficult virtue for us to achieve, especially when it has to be a balance between divine and human qualities. The Holy Spirit can achieve this balance.

Here are some guiding principles which may be helpful in detecting the presence of the Holy Spirit in human words and actions.

All that comes from the Holy Spirit bears the mark of humanity. This means that if a work has its origin in the inspiration of the Holy Spirit it will be divine, but at the same time it will be deeply human too. It cannot be otherwise, because in the person of Christ the Word of God has taken on flesh — divinity and humanity became one. All spiritual graces will somehow take on flesh in this world. Therefore a person who is really holy will be divine in the sense that he will be immersed in God; at the same time he will be human too. His supernatural sense and his humanity will develop together. Similarly, a doctrinal or teaching position is more likely to originate in an inspiration of the Spirit when it is marked by a balance between divine and human elements. For example, when someone presents a vision of the Church which points out all the divine qualities but obscures the humanity of the Church, his doctrine should be received with caution. Limitations, imperfections, and fallibility belong to the essence of the pilgrim Church nearly as much as its beauty, perfections, and infallibility. The true picture of the Church on earth is a balance of these opposing qualities.

The fruit of the Holy Spirit is usually a blend of old and new. It comes from an old tree but it has the fresh taste of this new season. We know that the fulness of the Gospel was given to the Apostles, but not the fulness of insight into the Gospel. Consequently, whenever there are new ideas and actions in the Church, they come from the Holy Spirit when they have their roots in tradition and at the same time contain new insights and new inspirations. When there is a balance between the old and new it is likely that the Holy Spirit is present. If there is no balance one can be reasonably sure that the Holy Spirit is absent.

Whatever comes from the Spirit of God is likely to manifest, in ordinary circumstances, a harmony between contemplation and action—that is, passivity in receiving God's inspiration and activity in building God's Kingdom. The reason is that God himself is eternal contemplation and he is seeing and enjoying the depths of his own divinity, while at the same time he is the eternally active God. The life of the Holy Trinity is dynamic: the

Son is being born from the Father, and the Holy
Spirit proceeds from the Father and the Son. God
also creates this world, and through his Spirit re-
creates it in Christ. Therefore all that comes from
God will be marked by a harmony between contemplation and action. Obviously there can be ex-
ceptions. It may well be that a person will be called
to contemplation only, though it is not likely that
a person will be called to action only. But either
of these would be extraordinary. In ordinary circumstances it is the harmony of both which demonstrates the presence of the Holy Spirit.

*Originality in thoughts and deeds can be a sign
of the presence of the Spirit.* Its absence may be
due to *his* absence. By originality I mean creative
ideas and actions, be it in a supernatural or a natural way. God is life and he gives life — more
abundant life. Originality is a manifestation of
life. Therefore a person who has the same ideas all
the time, who never revises his own opinion, is not
likely to be under the impact of the Holy Spirit.
Whenever the Spirit is there, some originality will
break through.

*Harmony between a spiritual vision and legal
wisdom is likely to point to the presence of the
Holy Spirit.* There are few things which are as op-
posed to each other as are spiritual intuition, with
its great freedom and personal character, and le-
galism, with its rigid rules that apply to general
situations and may become harmful to personal

needs. Many times in the history of the Church tensions arose between the Spirit and the law. Whenever, in the actions of a person, there is a harmony which demonstrates the dynamism and freedom of the Spirit together with a respect for the law, the person is likely to be under the impact of the Holy Spirit.

Increasing practicality can be a sign of developing sanctity. This may sound unusual, but since God made this world and knows it and loves it, whenever someone is on his way to a closer union with God he will become more and more practical in the administration of the problems of the world. Progress in holiness is not marked by dreaminess, but by greater shrewdness and common sense. St. Paul was a very practical person. One has only to recall how he organized a collection for the church of Jerusalem. The rule of St. Benedict has a mystical depth and a daily practicality. St. Teresa, the great contemplative, was one of the shrewdest women of her times, blessed with a great business sense.

All these signs and principles and their application to a given case with prudence and wisdom can serve as guide lines. They are necessary today because the individual Christian whether he is living in the world or in a religious house, will have to make many personal decisions. He will have to decide if a book really reflects the Spirit of Christ, if a periodical brings him the message of Good

News, if a lecturer is really talking in the Spirit. Let us recall, however, that better than any sign or principle the real guide in the life of the Christian should be the Holy Spirit himself. He should give him light and sympathy to see and to feel the presence of God's Spirit in others and in the whole world with all its events. Signs and principles are instruments toward this wisdom that cannot be put into words and that is truly a gift from God.

CONVERSION

Conversion is one of the great themes that dominate the biblical literature. Yahweh did not cease to ask his people to change their ways and to convert with their whole heart and mind to their God. In fact, Yahweh employed all the stratagems that a passionate friend knows. He attracted and encouraged, reproached and punished to achieve the desired result, the conversion of hearts.

The absolute condition for following Christ was a change of heart. Nothing else was enough. The change had to touch the internal man so deeply that he acquired a new personality. The Apostles themselves went out to proclaim that a new world has come in which men must live with a new heart.

At the origin of many great movements in our Christian history there was a conversion. A person was touched by the grace of God and under the impact of this touch his vision changed. It was enlarged and his small horizon, confined to his immediate needs, became immense with God's boundless plans. His hesitating steps were transformed into the sure tread of a giant.

Now what is this conversion so eminently desirable? Many good people, apparently not in need of it, say to their friends, "And pray for my conversion, too." The problem is worth exploring.

Let us begin by asking what is in the heart of the person who has been converted to God with that absoluteness that was first stated in the Decalogue and later perfected by Christ. "You must love the Lord your God with all your heart, with all your soul, with all your strength, and with all your mind, and your neighbor as yourself" (Luke 10:27). Such a person is a source of love, a wellspring of goodness for all.

It is difficult for us all to understand, not intellectually but existentially, what it means to be a wellspring of goodness. We have grown up in a commercial world where our everyday survival is based on the exchange of values: *quid pro quo*. Not only does money dominate the economy, but also the exchange of goods and services, the balance between work and income, service and reward are essential for the survival of the community.

To be a source of love or a wellspring of goodness is to enter into a different world. There is no exchange, there is no income and there is no profit. But there is a repeated, protracted, unceasing act of giving. One is reminded of the favorite topic of the Greek Fathers of the Church: the divinization of man. Man becomes like God, not intellectually by omniscience, not even by having some kind of power to work miracles, but by being as God is, a source of goodness. Out of that goodness the world was created and our life and death was assumed into the eternal plan of God.

When such a conversion has taken place in a man the question if one should love God first or man first vanishes meaninglessly. There are no firsts and seconds for the rays of the sun that reach the earth. They bring light and warmth to all creatures whether they are good or bad, beautiful or ugly, in blossom or in decay. All creation benefits from one source of goodness. Neither are there firsts and seconds for a man who lives and prospers on giving. His love reaches God as it reaches man, with one single undivided act. Who ever succeeded in dissecting the graceful abundance of a spring in the mountains? *One* is the source; *all* benefit from it according to their capacity. Or who ever succeeded in assigning priorities to the rays of the sun? It shines on all. Similarly, the goodness of a man converted to God reaches all, God and his neighbor. To argue whether one should find God in himself or through his neighbor is a false question. One should become a source of love, a wellspring of goodness. And then one will love God and neighbor with one act, one mind and one heart. Further distinctions in the practical order are superfluous.

A high ideal, admittedly. Who can really reach it? A new way of life. Who can achieve it? It is at this point that we have to be attentive. If we accept that we are contemplating the unreachable, the result may be disastrous. After all, not everybody is born to be a Don Quixote de la Mancha. Most of us do not have much talent for reaching after the unreachable. If conversion is an elusive aspiration but not a realistic proposition, we will decide to stay embedded in our small comfortable nest until, of course, a storm turns us out and threatens our life.

To be a source of love or a wellspring of goodness is a *reachable* ideal. But in the ordinary course of events it has to be reached bit by bit. History provides us with many dramatic, extraordinary conversions. The turning of Saul into Paul in the midst of mysterious signs of light and voices is probably the leading example. He has not been equaled even by St. Ignatius of Loyola, although the Basque knight's transformation was dramatic enough, too, the rough cannon ball and the gentle Virgin all playing their part. Yet for most earth-dwelling Christians conversion is an on-going process. We can become a source of love only once in a while. The realization that there is no reward for goodness can be a traumatic experience and we usually camouflage our hurt by righteous indignation and appeal to fair play and justice. Yet it is through such painful experience that our Christian personality grows and our heart is step-by-step changed and converted to God.

Traditionally there are many ways of training a Christian for greater maturity. Many literary minded saints left us methods to achieve progress toward a good life. A good method today would be to put the candidate for conversion, or call him the candidate for Christian maturity, into circumstances where he is compelled to give all and not receive anything. With some consistency the project should be designed in such a way that the first screams and protests of the candidate about the irrelevancy of the test provoke no redress. Granted, the method is unusual for our age. Yet it had a prominent place in Jesus' training of the Apostles. He found it hard to convey the idea to them that he had come to give and to give, even to the last drop of his blood. It took a long time for Peter and the Twelve to learn the same way of life. God knows (and we know) they did protest and they did what they could to run away from the task.

To be converted to God, then, means to be converted a little bit more every day with due allowance for ups and downs. The main trend should be upwards, but no one should take away the right of pilgrims to their weakness from time to time, provided that weakness is balanced by renewed strength.

Conversion is a reachable ideal. The very appearance of God among men in the person of Christ brings and proves that the unreachable is reachable. Besides Don Quixote hard-headed realists are invited: man can see, hear, touch and feel God. And because of this proximity to God the heart of man can be changed, day by day, and be filled with love and goodness. The sign of progress in this process is that the sharp distinctions between the love of God, of the neighbor, and of the world begin to fade away.

This world is in bad shape: it is difficult to argue otherwise. We all saw the picture of the mushroom-shaped cloud over Hiroshima, the cloud that marked our entrance into a new atomic age. We all experience the cruel agony of the tension that follows from social injustice and from benevolent indifference.

Is there anything that this world needs more than persons who have new hearts, who are sources of love, wellsprings of goodness for all creatures?